PRESENT PERFECT

Present Perfect Press
Melton Mowbray, UK
2022
All extracts are sourced from texts in the public domain
Cover image by Jared Subia
This publication has no official affiliation
© Jonathan Martin 2021
Terms and conditions:
The purchaser of this book is subject to the condition that he/she shall in no way resell it,
nor any part of it, nor make copies of it to distribute freely.

John Webster's

# The Duchess of Malfi

Translated into modern English

By J.M.Martin

## Introductory Note

This translation is based on the first quarto edition of *The Duchess of Malfi*, with modernised spellings.

The translation was written with ease of understanding at the forefront. One of the great things about Webster's writing is its tendency to be enigmatic, and whilst this translation has aimed to attribute accurate interpretations, any users of it should feel free to incline toward their own understandings. Comments such as the Cardinal's "wisdom begins at the end", for example, or Julia joining the "sweet delight and pretty excuse together" open themselves to a wide range of readings.

Writing this translation was an enjoyable challenge but did take quite a long time; I'd like to thank my dog Frank for keeping me company while I worked on it.

# DRAMATIS PERSONÆ

*The Duchess* – the ruler of the Italian town of Malfi. A widow.
*Ferdinand* – the Duke of Calabria, and the Duchess's twin brother.
*Cardinal* – brother of the Duchess and Ferdinand, and a cardinal in the Catholic church.
*Antonio* – the Duchess's steward (head servant).
*Bosola* – a criminal who works for the Cardinal.
*Cariola* – the Duchess's maid and friend.
*Delio* – a courtier and Antonio's friend.
*Castruchio* – a courtier in Malfi.
*Julia* – Castruchio's wife and the Cardinal's mistress.
*Malatesti* – a count.
*Pescara* – a marquis.
*Roderigo*, Silvio and Grisolan – courtiers.
An old lady, three children, several mad people, a doctor, two pilgrims.

## Act One

Scene One

[*Enter* ANTONIO *and* DELIO – *the court at Malfi.*]

  DEL: You are welcome to your country, dear Antonio;
You have been long in France, and you return
A very formal Frenchman in your habit:
How do you like the French court?

  ANT:    I admire it:
5 In seeking to reduce both state and people
To a fix'd order, their judicious king
Begins at home; quits first his royal palace
Of flattering sycophants, of dissolute
And infamous persons,—which he sweetly terms
10 His master's master-piece, the work of heaven;
Considering duly that a prince's court
Is like a common fountain, whence should flow
Pure silver drops in general, but if 't chance
Some curs'd example poison 't near the head,
15 Death and diseases through the whole land spread.
And what is 't makes this blessed government
But a most provident council, who dare freely
Inform him the corruption of the times?
Though some o' the court hold it presumption
20 To instruct princes what they ought to do,
It is a noble duty to inform them
What they ought to foresee. —Here comes Bosola,
The only court-gall' yet I observe his railing
Is not for simple love of piety:
25 Indeed, he rails at those things which he wants;
Would be as lecherous, covetous, or proud,

# SCENE ONE        MODERN

[*Enter* ANTONIO *and* DELIO – *the court at Malfi.*]

DELIO: Welcome back to Italy, my dear friend Antonio. You've been away in France for a long time, and you've come back dressed like a proper Frenchman. What did you think of the French court?

ANTONIO: I liked it.  To bring order to the government and the people, the sensible French king kicked out of his palace anyone who sucks up to him, and any people with loose morals or dodgy reputations, and says by managing his court this way he's following the example of God in His creation of the world.
Think of it like this: the political court is like a water fountain, from which pure, silver water should flow. But if by chance the head of that fountain (the king) becomes corrupted, then the fountain spreads death and disease to all who drink from it. What makes the king's government so blessed is the wise counsel from the advisors around him, who must be able to inform him freely and honestly, without fear of repercussions, of the bad things happening at the time. Some people in the court think it's arrogant to tell the king what he ought to do, but it is a good, noble thing to inform him of what he might need to anticipate.
— Here comes Bosola, the most bitter person in Malfi's court – but I notice he doesn't complain about everything simply because he has a feeling of moral superiority. Rather, he complains about the same things he desires for himself. He would be as lustful, greedy, proud violent and

Bloody, or envious, as any man,
If he had means to be so.—Here's the cardinal.

[*Enter* CARD: *and* BOSOLA]

BOS: I do haunt you still.
CARD:: So.
BOS: I have done you better service than to be slighted thus. Miserable age, where only the reward of doing well is the doing of it!

CARD:: You enforce your merit too much.
BOS: I fell into the galleys in your service: where, for two years together, I wore two towels instead of a shirt, with a knot on the shoulder, after the fashion of a Roman mantle. Slighted thus! I will thrive some way. Black-birds fatten best in hard weather; why not I in these dog-days?

CARD:: Would you could become honest!

BOS: With all your divinity do but direct me the way to it. I have known many travel far for it, and yet return as arrant knaves as they went forth, because they carried themselves always along with them. [*Exit* CARD:.] Are you gone? Some fellows, they say, are possessed with the devil, but this great fellow were able to possess the greatest devil, and make him worse.

ANT: He hath denied thee some suit?
BOS: He and his brother are like plum-trees that grow crooked over standing-pools; they are rich and o'erladen with fruit, but none but crows, pies, and caterpillars feed on them. Could I be one of their flattering panders, I would hang on their ears like a horseleech, till I were full, and then drop off. I pray, leave me. Who would rely upon these miserable dependencies, in expectation to be

jealous as the people he complains about if he had the chance. Here's the Cardinal.

[*Enter* CARDINAL *and* BOSOLA]

BOSOLA: Here I am, still following you around, waiting.
CARDINAL: So it seems.
BOSOLA: I've done good work for you and don't deserve to be insulted like this. What a miserable world, where the only reward for doing hard work is the doing of the work itself!
CARDINAL: You're praising yourself too much.
BOSOLA: My work for you landed me in a prison ship, where for two years I had to wear towels instead of a shirt and so ended up looking like a Roman woman. Where's my reward for all this? But I will get what I want somehow. Blackbirds get fattest in the winter, so why shouldn't I succeed in these rough times?
CARDINAL: I think you should focus on becoming a decent person.
BOSOLA: Use all your spiritual knowledge to tell me how. I've known many people who've gone off on journeys of self-improvement, but they returned the same scoundrels as they were when they departed, because they took themselves with them. (People can't change.)
You've gone? They say some people are possessed by the devil, but this Cardinal is so evil he could himself possess the devil, and make the devil more evil.

ANTONIO: The Cardinal has treated you unfairly?

BOSOLA: He and his brother Ferdinand are like crooked plum trees growing over a pond. Their branches are full of fruit (wealth), but they only share it with bad people. If I were one of their favourite people, one of the people who sucks up to them, I would feed on them until I were full and then drop away. You'd best leave me alone. What kind of person would allow themselves to become dependent on someone like the Cardinal just for the hope of being

advanc'd to-morrow? What creature ever fed worse than
hoping Tantalus? Nor ever died any man more fearfully
than he that hoped for a pardon.
60 There are rewards for hawks and dogs when they have
done us service; but for a soldier that hazards his limbs in
a battle, nothing but a kind of geometry is his last
supportation.

   DEL: Geometry?
   BOS: Ay, to hang in a fair pair of slings, take his latter
swing in the world upon an honourable pair of crutches,
65 from hospital to hospital. Fare ye well, sir: and yet do not
you scorn us; for places in the court are
but like beds in the hospital, where this man's head lies at
that man's foot, and so lower and lower.
[*Exit.*]

   DEL: I knew this fellow seven years in the galleys
70 For a notorious murder; and 'twas thought
The cardinal suborn'd it: he was releas'd
By the French general, Gaston de Foix,
When he recover'd Naples.
   ANT: 'Tis great pity
He should be thus neglected: I have heard
75 He 's very valiant. This foul melancholy
Will poison all his goodness; for, I 'll tell you,
If too immoderate sleep be truly said
To be an inward rust unto the soul,
If then doth follow want of action
80 Breeds all black malcontents; and their close rearing,
Like moths in cloth, do hurt for want of wearing.

rewarded at some unknown point in the future? What person has ever felt more starved than Tantalus, who reached desperately for the food and drink offered before him, only to have it constantly pulled away? No person has died a more dreadful death than the criminal who endlessly hopes his crimes might one day be forgiven.

Animals are rewarded when they help us, but when soldiers risk their limbs in a battle their only reward is geometry.

DELIO: Err...geometry...?
BOSOLA: Yes, the geometry of the slings and crutches they have to use for the rest of their lives to support their broken limbs while they go stumbling from hospital to hospital. Goodbye, sir, and don't think I am lesser than you. In the political court, people stand with their feet on other people's heads (like in hospital where their feet lie by others' heads) to try and raise their status, but instead we all sink lower and lower together. [Exit.]
DELIO: I've heard this Bosola spent seven years on a prison ship as punishment for a murder which, according to rumour, had been ordered by the Cardinal. They say Bosola was released by a famous French general when he helped in the battle for Naples.
ANTONIO: It seems a great shame Bosola should be treated that way by the Cardinal. I've heard he's very brave. His bad mood will spoil all his good qualities, because – allow me to explain – if it's true that too much sleep is bad for the soul, then it makes sense that a lack of purpose in our lives makes people miserable, just like a piece of clothing that's not worn and ends up eaten by moths.

ORIGINAL  ACT ONE

### WHAT'S GOING ON?
*Antonio is the Duchess's steward — which is like a chief servant. He's just come back from a trip to France, and can't stop going on about how impressed he was with the French court. "Court" is an important thing in this play — it was the place, often in a palace, where the sovereign such as the king or duchess etc. would preside over political dealings. The court was comprised of courtiers — members of the nobility, members of the sovereign's household, knights, followers, clergy, etc., who often wrangled to get close to the sovereign in order to exert influence and/or receive reward. Much of*

[*Enter* ANTONIO. DELIO, FERDINAND, CASTRUCHIO, SILVIO.]
DEL: The presence 'gins to fill: you promis'd me
To make me the partaker of the natures
Of some of your great courtiers.
ANT:           The Lord Cardinal's,
85 And other strangers, that are now in court?
I shall: here comes the great Calabrian Duke.
FERD: Who took the ring oftenest?
SIL: Antonio Bologna, my lord.
FERD: Our sister Duchess' great master of her household: Give him the jewel. When shall we leave this
90 sportive action, and fall to action indeed?

CAST: Methinks, my lord, you should not desire to go to war in person.
FERD: Now, for some gravity; why, my lord?
CAST: It is fitting a soldier arise to be a prince, but not
95 necessary a prince descend to be a captain.

FERD: No?

SCENE ONE                    MODERN

*this play, including the opening, focuses on the Duchess's court. Bosola seeks to climb the hierarchy of the court.*

*Antonio was clearly struck by the lack of corruption in the French court, which Webster uses to highlight the contrast of this court. There's gossip; rumours of dark deeds; bitterness over lack of payment; immorality in a high-ranking member of the Catholic church — all in the first couple of pages!*

*While Bosola is full of scorn for the immorality of the court, he nevertheless longs to be part of it himself. He's desperate for the reward of promotion which he feels his patron (employer) the Cardinal owes him.*

[*Enter* ANTONIO. DELIO, FERDINAND, CASTRUCHIO, SILVIO.]

DELIO: The place is filling up with people. You promised to tell me about these courtiers.

ANTONIO: About the Cardinal, and other people? I will. Here comes the great Duke of Calabria, Ferdinand.

FERDINAND: Who won the jousting competition?
SILVIO: Antonio did.

FERDINAND: Antonio, my sister's steward. Then give him the jewel as his prize. Now, when shall we stop talking about sport and start talking about real action? ["Action" here likely refers to war, but, as with the "ring" comment above, also carries the possibility of sexual innuendo.]
CASTRUCHIO: I think, my lord, you shouldn't want to take part in the war in person.
FERDINAND: Now for some serious talk. Why shouldn't I?
CASTRUCHIO: It's perfectly proper for a soldier to raise his status to a prince, but not for a prince to lower his status to that of a soldier.
FERDINAND: No?

CAST: No, my lord;
He were far better do it by a deputy.

FERD: Why should he not as well sleep, or eat by a deputy?
100 This might take idle, offensive, and base office from him,
Whereas the other deprives him of honour.
CAST: Believe my experience: that realm is never long in quiet, where the ruler is a soldier.

FERD: Thou toldest me
105 Thy wife could not endure fighting.
CAST: True, my lord.
FERD: And of a jest she broke of a captain
she met full of wounds: I have forgot it.
CAST: She told him, my lord, he was a pitiful fellow, to
110 lie like the children of Ismael, all in tents.

FERD: Why, there's a wit were able to undo
All the chirugeons o'th' city, for although gallants should
quarrel, and had drawn their weapons, and were ready to
go to it, yet her persuasions would make them put up.

115 CAST: That she would, my lord.
How do you like my Spanish gennet?

RODERIGO: He is all fire.

FERD: I am of Pliny's opinion, I think he was begot by the wind; he runs as if he were ballassed with quicksilver.

120 SLIVIO: True, my lord, he reels from the tilt often.
ROD. And GRIS.: Ha, ha, ha!

FERD: Why do you laugh? methinks you that are courtiers should be my touchwood, take fire when I give fire; that is, not laugh but when I laugh, were the subject
125 never so witty.

SCENE ONE　　　　　MODERN

CASTRUCHIO: No, it would be better for the prince to have someone represent him on the battlefield: a deputy to fight in his place.

FERDINAND: Then the prince might as well have a deputy to sleep and eat for him, which would indeed save the prince from some dull, idle duties. But having a deputy in battle would deprive the prince of honour.

CASTRUCHIO: In my experience, the country whose ruler is also a soldier is never a peaceful country.

FERDINAND: You told me your wife couldn't tolerate fighting.

CASTRUCHIO: That's true, my lord.

FERDINAND: And you told me of a joke she made about a wounded soldier, but I can't remember it.

CASTRUCHIO: She told this soldier he was pathetic for lying around like people who live in deserts, all in tents. ["Tents" also meant bandages.]

FERDINAND: She has a wit capable of ruining all the surgeons in the city — because young lads, all ready to fight each other over a woman and ready to cut each other up, could be persuaded to shut up by her wit.

CASTRUCHIO. That's true, my lord. What do you think of my new horse?

RODERIGO: He looks fiery.

FERDINAND: I think your horse looks as if its mother was impregnated by the wind, as was what the philosopher Pliny said happened with horses, and he runs as if mercury ran through his blood, keeping him balanced.

SILVIO: That's true — he runs away from the action quickly.

RODRIGO and GRISOLAN: Ha ha ha! [They likely detect sexual innuendo in Silvio's comment.]

FERDINAND: You two - why are you laughing? It is my opinion that you courtiers should follow my lead — you should be like tinder in a fire, only igniting when the fire gives you flame — meaning, don't laugh until I laughed. [A

CAST: True, my lord; I myself have heard a very good jest, and have scorned to seem to have so silly a wit, as to understand it.

FERD: But I can laugh at your fool, my lord.

130  CAST: He cannot speak, you know, but he makes faces: my lady cannot abide him.

FERD: No?

CAST: Nor endure to be in merry company; for she says too much laughing, and too much company, fills her too
135 full of the wrinkle.

FERD: I would then have a mathematical instrument made for her face, that she might not laugh out of compass. I shall shortly visit you at Milan, Lord Silvio.

SIL: Your grace shall arrive most welcome.

140  FERD: You are a good horseman, Antonio: you have excellent riders in France: what do you think of good horsemanship?

ANT: Nobly, my lord: as out of the Grecian horse issued many famous princes, so out of brave horsemanship
145 Arise the first sparks of growing resolution, that raise the mind to noble action.

FERD: You have bespoke it worthily.

---

### WHAT'S GOING ON?

*Ferdinand, the Duchess's twin brother and a Duke, is introduced as the antithesis of the French king Antonio raved about. Whereas the king believed in being surrounded by*

---

SIL: Your brother, the lord Cardinal, and sister Duchess.

SCENE ONE — MODERN

tense pause, then Ferdinand himself laughs.] Unless the joke was as funny as this one.

CASTRUCHIO: That's true, my lord. I myself have often heard what I thought was a good joke, but thought it best not to laugh in case I seemed simpleminded for liking it.

FERDINAND: But I can laugh at something as simple as your fool (jester).

CASTRUCHIO: My fool can't speak, you know, but he does make funny faces. My wife can't stand him.

FERDINAND: No?

CASTRUCHIO: Nor can she tolerate being in merry company, because she thinks too much laughing will make her face wrinkled.

FERDINAND: In that case I'll have a special instrument made for her face to prevent her laughing in a messy way that. that will spoil her appearance. I'll visit you soon at Milan, Silvio.

SILVIO: You'll be most welcome.

FERDINAND: You are a good horseman, Antonio, and you must have seen excellent riders in France. What do you think about good horsemanship?

ANTONIO: I think it is a noble thing. Just as many famous princes emerged from the Trojan horse in their assault on Troy, from brave horsemanship emerges a sense of resolution that helps the mind to drive noble actions.

FERDINAND: You speak of it in a worthy way.

---

*honest advisors and banishing flatterers, Ferdinand wants those around him to model themselves on him. The talk of sport, rings, action, etc. brings a level of sexual innuendo that hints at Ferdinand's perverse nature.*

---

SILVIO: Here comes your brother the Cardinal, and your sister the Duchess.

ORIGINAL             ACT ONE

[*Enter* CARD:, DUCHESS, CARIOLA, *and* JULIA.]

    CARD:: Are the gallies come about?
150 GRISOLAN: They are, my lord.
    FERD: Here's the Lord Silvio is come to take his leave.
    DEL: [Aside] Now, sir, your promise: what's that
    Cardinal? I mean his temper? They say he's a brave fellow,
    Will play his five thousand crowns at tennis, dance,
155 Court ladies, and one that hath fought single combats.
    ANT: Some such flashes superficially hang on him, for
form; but observe his inward character: he is a
melancholy churchman; the spring in his face is nothing
but the engendering of toads; where he is jealous of any
160 man, he lays worse plots for him than ever was imposed
on
Hercules, for he strews in his way flatterers, panders,
intelligencers, atheists, and a thousand such political
monsters. He should have been Pope, but instead
of coming to it by the primitive decency of the church, he
165 did bestow bribes so largely, and so impudently, as if he
would have carried it away withou heaven's knowledge.
some good he hath done-

    DEL: You have given too much of him: what's his
brother?

    ANT: The duke there? a most perverse and turbulent
nature:
170 What appears in him mirth is merely outside;
If he laugh heartily, it is to laugh
All honesty out of fashion.

    DEL: Twins?
    ANT: In quality.
He speaks with others' toungues, and hears men's suits
With others' ears; will seem to sleep o' th' bench
175 Only to entrap offenders in their answers;

SCENE ONE                    MODERN

[*Enter* CARDINAL, DUCHESS, CARIOLA, *and* JULIA.]

CARDINAL: Have the battleships returned?
GRISOLAN: Yes.
FERDINAND: Silvio is leaving us.
DELIO: [*Aside*] Now Antonio, you promised to tell me about the Cardinal. What's he like? Rumour is he's quite outlandish – that he gambles, dances, romances women, and gets in fights.
ANTONIO: Yes, but that's not really important. Those are just superficial things. Consider his inner nature: he is dark-tempered for a religious person; the apparent freshness of his face hides corruption, like foul toads emerging from a merry stream. If he becomes jealous of someone, he'll destroy that person with cunning plots worse than any faced by Hercules. He surrounds himself with people who flatter and suck up to him, and with spies, and other ungodly people. He could have been the Pope, but instead of raising his status in the legitimate way, he gave out massive bribes , carelessly and disrespectfully, acting as if he could have taken what he wanted without punishment from God. Lots of good he's done [said sarcastically].

DELIO: You've said too much about him. What about his brother, Ferdinand?

ANTONIO: The Duke? He has a perverse and unstable nature. He might look merry, but it's only on the outside. Nothing he does is honest or sincere.


DELIO: So he's just as bad as the Cardinal?
ANTONIO: Yes. Ferdinand always puts on an act, never speaking with his own voice but imitating others. He's deceptive – he'll pretend he's not listening, and then use people's words against them. He isn't interested in fair

Dooms men to death by information,
Rewards by hearsay.

  DEL: Then the law to him
Is like a foul black cobweb to a spider,
He makes it his dwelling and a prison
To entangle those shall feed him.
  ANT: Most true:
He never pays debts unless they be shrewd turns,
And those he will confess that he doth owe.
Last, for his brother there, the cardinal,
They that do flatter him most say oracles
Hang at his lips; and verily I believe them,
For the devil speaks in them.
But for their sister, the right noble duchess,
You never fix'd your eye on three fair medals
Cast in one figure, of so different temper.
For her discourse, it is so full of rapture,
You only will begin then to be sorry
When she doth end her speech, and wish, in wonder,
She held it less vain-glory, to talk much,
Than your penance to hear her: whilst she speaks,
She throws upon a man so sweet a look,
That it were able to raise one to a galliard
That lay in a dead palsy, and to dote
On that sweet countenance; but in that look
There speaketh so divine a continence,
As cuts off all lascivious and vain hope.
Her days are practis'd in such noble virtue,
That sure her nights, nay more, her very sleeps,
Are more in heaven, than other ladies' shrifts.
Let all sweet ladies break their flattering glasses,
And dress themselves in her.
  DEL: Fie, Antonio,
You play the wire-drawer with her commendation.
  ANT: I'll case the picture up: only thus much,
All her particular worth, grows to this sum;
She stains the time past, lights the time to come.

## SCENE ONE  MODERN

justice — he punishes and rewards people on the basis of information or gossip that may not be true.
DELIO: Oh, then he uses the law like a trap. Like a spider's web, the law for Ferdinand is a home and a prison, in which he traps his victims.

ANTONIO: That's true. He never pays his debts unless by doing so he can manipulate someone, and otherwise he won't admit to owing any debt. Finally, about his brother the Cardinal, his biggest suck ups think that a god-like power speaks through his lips, and truly I believe them, because the devil speaks through the Cardinal's lips.
But about their sister, the noble Duchess — you have never seen three things, all related to each other, of such different qualities. Her speech is so full of intense joy
that you will be sorry when it stops, and you'll wish she didn't think it vain to talk a lot.

She looks at who she's speaking to so sweetly that it could make a dying person leap up and dance, and gaze at her face with adoration. But in that look there is a self-control that cuts of all lustful thoughts in the person being looked at. She spends her days in such a noble, virtuous manner that makes her more pure in her sleep than other women at confession. Other women should break their mirrors and use her as their reflection to model themselves after.

DELIO: Blimey, Antonio, enough. You're stringing out your praise for her a bit much.
ANTONIO: I'll summarise it like this: she is like a great, powerful light that shines hope and goodness on the future while casting shadow over the past and all that is behind.

ACT ONE

210  CARI: You must attend my lady in the gallery,
Some half an hour hence.
   ANT:            I shall.
                              [*Exeunt* Antonio *and* Delio.]
FERD: Sister, I have a suit to you.
DUCH: To me, sir?
   FERD: A gentleman here, Daniel de Bosola,
One that was in the gallies-
   DUCH: Yes, I know him.
215  FERD: A worthy fellow h'is: pray let me entreat for the
provisorship of your horse.
   DUCH: Your knowledge of him
Commends him and prefers him.
   FERD: Call him hither.
                              [*Exit* Attendant.]
We are now upon parting.- Good Lord Silvio,
Do us commend to all our noble friens
220  At the leaguer.
   SIL: Sir, I shall.
   FERD: You are for Milan?
   SIL: I am.
   DUCH: Bring the carroches: we'll bring you down to
the haven.

   [*Exeunt all but the* CARD: *and* FERDINAND.]
   CARD:: Be sure you entertain that Bosola
For your intelligence: I would not be seen in't;
225  And therefore many times I have slighted him,
When he did court our furtherance, as this morning.
   FERD: Antonio, the great master of her household,
Had been far fitter.
   CARD:: You are deceiv'd in him:
His nature is too honest for such business.
230  He comes: I'll leave you

                              [*Exit* Cardinal.]

## SCENE ONE  MODERN

CARIOLA: Antonio, the Duchess wants to see you, in the gallery, in thirty minutes.
ANTONIO: I'll be there.
                      [*Exeunt* ANTONIO *and* DELIO:]
FERDINAND: Sister, I have something of interest to you.
DUCHESS: To me, sir?
FERDINAND: This gentleman, Daniel de Bosola, who spent time in the galleys —
DUCHESS: Yes, I've heard of him.
FERDINAND: He's a good man. Please let me recommend him for the position of your stableman.
DUCHESS: I trust your recommendation.

FERDINAND: Bring Bosola here.
                      [*Exit* Attendant *to fetch* BOSOLA.]
Soon we will part ways. Silvio, give our greetings to the soldiers at the battle-camp.

SILVIO: I will.
FERDINAND: Are you going to Milan?
SILVIO: I am.
DUCHESS: Bring the carriages; we'll take you to the harbour.
    [*Exeunt all but the* CARDINAL *and* FERDINAND.]
CARDINAL: Make sure to use that Bosola as a spy. I can't be seen to have anything to do with it, which is why I speak rudely to him, when he's after me for his reward, such as this morning.
FERDINAND: Antonio, her steward, would be a better spy.

CARDINAL: You're wrong about him. He's too honest for such dirty business. Here he comes; I'll leave you alone.

                              [*Exit* CARDINAL.]

[Enter BOSOLA.]

BOS: I was lur'd to you.

FERD: My brother here, the cardinal could never
Abide you.

BOS: Never since he was in my debt.

FERD: May be some oblique character in your face
Made him suspect you.

BOS: Doth he study physiognomy?
There's no more credit to be given to th' face,
Than to a sick man's urine, which some call
The physician's whore, because she cozens him.
He did suspect me wrongfully.

FERD: For that
You must give great men leave to take their times.
Distrust doth cause us seldom be deceiv'd:
You see, the oft shaking of the cedar-tree
Fastens it more at root.

BOS: Yet, take heed;
For to suspect a friend unworthily,
Instructs him the next way to suspect you,
And prompts him to deceive you.

FERD: There's gold.

BOS: So,
What follows? never rain'd such showers as these
Without thunderbolts i' th' tail of them: whose throat must I cut?

FERD: Your inclination to shed blood rides post
Before my occasion to use you. I give you that
To live i'th' court here, and observe the duchess;
To note all the particulars of her 'haviour,
What suitors do solicit her for marriage,
And whom she best affects. She's a young widow:
I would not have her marry again.

BOS: No, sir?

SCENE ONE       MODERN

[*Enter* BOSOLA.]

BOSOLA: I was lured into coming to see you.
FERDINAND: My brother, the Cardinal, can't stand you.

BOSOLA: Because he owes me.
FERDINAND: Maybe something about your appearance makes him suspicious of you.
BOSOLA: Is he an expert on facial expressions? The face says no more about a person than urine says about a sick person's illness. Urine is like a doctor's prostitute, because it deceives him. The Cardinal is wrong to be suspicious of me.

FERDINAND: You must allow great men to be cautious. People who don't trust others won't be deceived by others. Cedar trees get stronger the more they are shaken. [This analogy parallels the disturbance of a tree in the wind to the inner disturbance of a suspicious person's mind — both result in more strength.]
BOSOLA: But be warned — if you're suspicious of a friend without reason, then you encourage the friend to be suspicious of you and he will be more likely to deceive you.

FERDINAND: Here's some gold for you.
BOSOLA: What's the catch? Offers of gold don't come without some sort of corruption. Who must I kill?

FERDINAND: Your strange inclination to kill people is not the reason I have decided to use you. I instruct you to live here in the Duchess's court and to watch her; watch all the particulars of her behaviour, what men are interested in marrying her, and what men she likes most. She is a young widow and I do not want her to marry again.

BOSOLA: Why not?

FERD: Do not you ask the reason; but be satisfied
I say I would not.
  BOS: It seems you would create me
One of your familiars.


  FERD: Familiar! what's that?
  BOS: Why, a very quaint invisible devil in flesh;
260 As intelligencer.
  FERD: Such a kind of thriving thing
I would wish thee; and ere long, thou may'st arrive
At a higher place by't.
  BOS: Take your devils,
Which hell calls angels: these curs'd gifts would make
You a corrupter, me an impudent traitor;
265 And should I take these, they'd take me to hell.
  FERD: Sir, I'll take nothing from you, that I have given:
There is a place that I procur'd for you
This morning, the provisorship o'th'horse;
Have you heard on't?
  BOS: No.
  FERD: 'Tis yours: is't not worth thanks?
270 BOS: I would have you curse yourself now, that your bounty
(Which makes men truly noble) e'er should make
Me a villain. O, that to avoid ingratitude
For the good deed you have done me, I must do
All the ill man can invent! Thus the devil
275 Candies all sins o'er; and what heaven terms vile
That names he complemental.

  FERD: Be yourself;
Keep your old garb of melancholy; 'twill express
You envy those that stand above your reach,
Yet strive not to come near 'em: this will gain
280 Access to private lodgings, where yourself
May, like a politic dormouse-

## SCENE ONE  MODERN

FERDINAND: Don't ask why; just be satisfied that I say I do not want it.
BOSOLA: It seems you would make me one of your familiars. [This refers to a witch's familiar – a demon in the form of an animal.]
FERDINAND: What do you mean?
BOSOLA: A devil in the form of a creature – a spy.

FERDINAND: Yes, that's what I want you to be, and before long you'll be rewarded for it with promotion to a higher status.
BOSOLA: Take your devilish money ["angels" here is an allusion to a type of gold coin known as the "angel coin"]. If I accept your offer, I will become a traitor and you will be corrupted; if I accept, I will end up in hell.
FERDINAND: Sir, I'm not going to take from you the money I've already said is yours. I've got you a job working for the Duchess as her stableman. Have you heard about it?

BOSOLA: No.
FERDINAND: Well it's yours. Is that not worth thanks?
BOSOLA: I want you to curse yourself because the reward you offer me of status, which makes most men noble, will make me a villain. Oh, that to avoid seeming ungrateful for the good deed you have done me, I must do evil. You do what the devil does – make sin seem sweet, and call good what heaven calls vile.

FERDINAND: Fine, then keep being your normal self: keep wearing your normal costume of misery; it will show how you envy people of higher status and do nothing to try and reach their status. Or, take this job, which will give you access to the Duchess's private lodgings, where you may, like a cunning dormouse –

BOS: As I have seen some,
Feed in a lord's dish, half asleep, not seeming
To listen to any talk; and yet these rogues
Have cut his throat in a dream. What's my place?
285 The provisorship o'th' horse? say, then, my corruption
Grew out of horse-dung: I am your creature.

FERD: Away.
BOS: Let good men, for good deeds, covet good fame,
Since place and riches, oft are bribes of shame:
290 Sometimes the devil doth preach.

[*Exit* Bosola.]

### WHAT'S GOING ON?
*Ferdinand employs Bosola to spy on the Duchess, because both Ferdinand and the Cardinal are concerned about the possibility of her remarrying (the Duchess is a widow). The next section gives more clue about why they're so concerned.*

[*Enter* DUCHESS, CARD:, *and* CARIOLA.]
CARD:: We are to part from you; and your own discretion
Must now be your director.

FERD: You are a widow:
You know already what man is; and therefore
Let not youth, high promotion, eloquence-
295 CARD:: No,
Nor anything without the addition, honour,
Sway your high blood.

FERD: Marry! they are most luxurious,
Will wed twice.
CARD:: O, fie!
FERD: Their livers are more spotted
Than Laban's sheep.

SCENE ONE          MODERN

BOSOLA: Like the rogues I've seen who eat their lord's food, seeming innocent, half asleep and not listening, and dream of cutting their lord's throat. What's my job? Stableman? Then say my journey to corruption began by growing out of horse-dung. I reluctantly accept. I am your monster.

FERDINAND: Now go.

BOSOLA: Good men can desire good reputation as a reward for doing good deeds, but I must do shameful things for the reward of status and wealth, as the devil teaches.

[*Exit* BOSOLA.]

---

*Bosola's acceptance of the job illuminates his internal conflict – he is aware he's agreeing to do something immoral, and is repulsed by this, but he desires the rewards of status and wealth dangled before him.*

---

[*Enter* DUCHESS, CARDINAL, *and* CARIOLA.]

CARDINAL: [to the Duchess] Ferdinand and I are leaving you, so you must now be led by your own good sense.

FERDINAND: You are a widow, so you've had experience with men and know what they're like; therefore don't be tempted by any youthful, high status, sweet talking man –

CARDINAL: No, don't let any dishonourable, low-class man pollute your high-class blood.

FERDINAND: Only the most lustful people get married twice.

CARDINAL: Oh, do stop!

FERDINAND: They are as over-indulgent as alcoholics, with livers even more spotted than the spotted sheep of Laban in the Bible.

DUCH: Diamonds are of most value,
They say, that have past through most jewellers' hands.

300 FERD: Whores, by that rule, are precious.

DUCH: Will you hear me?
I'll never marry.
CARD:: So most widows say;
But commonly that motion lasts no longer
Than the turning of an hour-glass: the funeral sermon
And it, end both together.
FERD: Now hear me:
305 You live in a rank pasture here, i'th' court;
There is a kind of honey-dew that's deadly;
'Twill poison your fame; look to't: be not cunning;
For they whose faces do belie their hearts,
Are witches ere they arrive at twenty years,
310 Ay, and give the devil suck.

DUCH: This is terrible good counsel.

FERD: Hypocrisy is woven of a fine small thread,
Subtler than Vulcan's engine: yet, believ't,
Your darkest actions, nay, your privat'st thoughts,
Will come to light.
CARD:: You may flatter yourself,
315 And take your own choice; privately be married
Under the eaves of night-
FERD: Think't the best voyage
That e'er you made; like the irregular crab,
Which, though't goes backward, thinks that it goes right,
Because it goes its own way: but observe,
320 Such weddings may more properly be said
To be executed, than celebrated.

SCENE ONE          MODERN

DUCHESS: They say the most valuable diamonds (women) are the ones that have passed through most jewellers' (men's) hands.
FERDINAND: By that rule prostitutes are valuable.
DUCHESS: Will you listen to me? I will not marry again.

CARDINAL: Which is what most widows say, but often that notion lasts no longer than an hour — the same time as a funeral sermon.

FERDINAND: Listen to me: you live in a place full of temptation here in the court,
an overgrown excess of tempting young men; they are a sweet but deadly honey that will destroy your good reputation. Listen: don't try and get away with doing something in secret, because women who try to deceive end up looking like witches before they're twenty years old, and become more corrupted, feeding the devil at their breast.

DUCHESS: This is great advice [very sarcastic — note the "terrible good" oxymoron].

FERDINAND: Deceitfulness is subtle and hard to spot — just as invisible as the net Vulcan used to catch his cheating wife — but nevertheless believe that your most private deeds and thoughts will be exposed.
CARDINAL: You may please yourself, and do what you want — have a secret wedding —

FERDINAND: You might think of such a wedding as the best journey you ever made and a good choice because it's your own choice, but it will be the wrong choice — just like the crab who makes the choice to go in one direction, because he thinks it's the right one, but he's walking sideways, so ends up going in the wrong direction. Such weddings aren't celebrated so much as executed [note the dual meaning of this last word].

CARD:: The marriage night
Is the entrance into some prison.
   FERD: And those joys,
Those lustful pleasures, are like heavy sleeps
Which do forerun man's mischief.
   CARD:: Fare you well.
325 Wisdom begins at the end: remember it.

[*Exit* Cardinal.]

   DUCH: I think this speech between you both was studied,
It came so roundly off.
   FERD: You are my sister;
This was my father's poinard, do you see?
I'd be loath to see't look rusty, 'cause 'twas his.
330 I would have you to give o'er these chargeable revels,
A visor and a mask are whispering rooms That were never built for goodness;- fare ye well,
And beware that part, which like the lamprey,
Hath never a bone in't.
   DUCH: Fie, sir.
   FERD: Nay,
335 I mean the tongue; variety of courtship;
What cannot a neat knave with a smooth tale
Make a woman believe: Farewell, lusty widow.

[*Exit* Ferdinand.]

   DUCH: Shall this move me? If all my royal kindred
Lay in my way unto this marriage,
340 I'd make them my low footsteps; and even now,
Even in this hate, as men in some great battles,
By apprehending danger, have achiev'd
Almost impossible actions,- I have heard soldiers say so,-
So I through frights and threatenings will assay
345 This dangerous venture. Let old wives report
I wink'd, and chose a husband.Cariola,

## SCENE ONE    MODERN

CARDINAL: Getting married is like entering a prison.
FERDINAND: And the sexual pleasures of marriage are sinful, like the pleasant heavy sleep of a dead man before he goes to hell.

CARDINAL: Farewell, and remember this: wisdom begins by thinking about what the final consequences of our actions might be.
    [*Exit* CARDINAL]
DUCHESS: The speech you've both given sounded rehearsed.

FERDINAND: You are my sister. This was my father's dagger, you see it? [*Waves a dagger about in front of her.*] I'd hate for it to get rusty, because it was his. I want you to give up these flashy masquerades (parties where people wear masks) because people can be deceitful behind their masks. Goodbye, and beware of that part (of a man's body) which, like the eel, doesn't have a bone in it.

DUCHESS: Please stop [disgusted].
FERDINAND: What?! I was talking about the tongue! A scoundrel with a sweet tongue can deceive any woman. Goodbye, lusty widow.

                            [*Exit* FERDINAND.]
DUCHESS: Was that supposed to impress me? If all my royal relations were to oppose my marriage, I would just step over them. Even in this hate being shown toward me, I will go ahead like men in great battles — I have heard they achieve almost impossible successes by being alert to danger, and so by being alert to these fears and threats made toward me I too can succeed in the dangerous venture of marriage. Let gossips say I chose a husband without care or reason for all I care. Cariola,

ORIGINAL ACT ONE

To thy known secrecy I have given up
More than my life- my fame.

CARI: Both shall be safe:
For I'll conceal this secret from the world,
350 As warily as those that trade in poison
Keep poison from their children.

DUCH: Thy protestation
Is ingenious and hearty: I believe it.
Is Antonio come?

CARI: He attends you.
DUCH: Good dear soul,
Leave me; but place thyself behind the arras,
355 Where thou may'st overhear us. Wish me good speed,
For I am going into a wilderness
Where I shall find no path, nor friendly clew,
To be my guide.

[*Exit* CARIOLA.]

### WHAT'S GOING ON?
*The Cardinal and Ferdinand fulfil familiar patriarchal roles of exerting male authority over a woman's independent marriage choices, but with a degree of hyperbole that makes such authority seem near comically ridiculous even to a Jacobean audience. The Cardinal is clearly concerned the Duchess may marry someone of low social standing and compromise the "honour" of the family. Ferdinand's motivation is less explicitly clear, but all his talk of sex and*

[*Enter* ANTONIO.]

DUCH: I sent for you: sit down;
Take pen and ink, and write: are you ready?
ANT: Yes.
360 DUCH: What did I say?
ANT: That I should write somewhat.
DUCH: O, I remember.

SCENE ONE                    MODERN

I'm sharing with you a secret and by doing so I am trusting you with my reputation — which is more important than my life.
CARIOLA: Both your life and reputation will be safe, because I'll keep this secret (your marriage) from the world as carefully as poison-sellers keep their children safe from poison.
DUCHESS: You speak cleverly and whole-heartedly; I believe you. Has Antonio come?

CARIOLA: He's waiting for you.
DUCHESS: Good dear soul, leave me, but hide behind the screen, where you can listen to us. Wish me well, because I am going into a wilderness where nothing is familiar and there is no trail to guide me.

---

*desire is a reasonable indication of his own incestuous desire toward the Duchess his twin sister, and jealousy toward any man she might wish to marry. The dagger indicates the lethal threat of his jealousy, but also serves as a phallic symbol of his (violent) desire. The good old Duchess, though — she's immediately dismissive of her brothers — perhaps rather naively — and resolves to do what she wants.*

---

[CARIOLA *goes behind a screen. Enter* ANTONIO.]
DUCHESS: I sent for you: sit down; take up a pen and write. Are you ready?
ANTONIO: Yes.
DUCHESS: What was I saying?
ANTONIO: That I should write something.
DUCHESS: Oh, I remember.

31

After these triumphs and this large expense,
It's fit, like thrifty husbands, we inquire
What's laid up for to-morrow.

365 ANT: So please your beauteous excellence.
   DUCH: Beauteous! Indeed I thank you:
I look young for your sake;
You have ta'en my cares upon you.
   ANT: I'll fetch your grace
The particulars of your revenue and expence.
   DUCH: O, you are
An upright treasurer; but you mistook:
370 For when I said I meant to make inquiry
What's laid up for to-morrow, I did mean
What's laid up yonder for me.
   ANT: Where?
   DUCH: In heaven.
I am making my will, (as 'tis fit princes should,
In perfect memory, ) and, I pray, sir, tell me
375 Were not one better make it smiling, thus,
Than in deep groans, and terrible ghastly looks,
As if the gifts we parted with procur'd
That violent distraction?
   ANT: O, much better.
   DUCH: If I had a husband now, this care were quit:
380 But I intend to make you overseer.
What good deed shall we first remember? say.

ANT: Begin with that first good deed begun i'th'world
After man's creation, the sacrament of marriage:
I'd have you first provide for a good husband;
385 Give him all.
   DUCH: All?
   ANT: Yes, your excellent self.

After spending lots of money on parties and entertainments, it's important we go through the books and see how much we've got left for the future. Like a husband — I mean, a manager of the household — who's careful with what's spent.
ANTONIO: If it pleases your beauteous excellence.
DUCHESS: Beauteous! Indeed I thank you. That I still I look young is thanks to you: you take the weight of my troubles off me.
ANTONIO: I'll fetch for your Grace the details of your finances — your savings and expenses.
DUCHESS: Oh, you are an upstanding accountant, but you're mistaken: when I said I meant to think about what's in store in the future, I meant what's in store up there.

ANTONIO: Where?

DUCHESS: In heaven. I am making my will, as it's proper for princes to do, if I remember rightly. Please sir, tell me, isn't it better to make it when I'm happy, like now, rather than wait until we're all miserable and groaning, as if it caused us great pain to part with the gifts we promise in our will?

ANTONIO: You're right; it's much better like this.
DUCHESS: If I had a husband, I wouldn't have to worry about making a will, but I intend to put you in charge of it. Who should be mentioned first in it? Tell me.
ANTONIO: You should start with the first good thing that came with the creation of people: marriage. I think you should provide for your next husband, whoever he may be. in your will. Give him everything.
DUCHESS: Everything?
ANTONIO: Yes — give him yourself.

DUCH: In a winding sheet?

ANT: In a couple.

  DUCH: St. Winifred, that were a strange will!
  ANT: 'Twere strange if there were no will in you
To marry again.

DUCH: What do you think of marriage?
390  ANT: I take't, as those that deny purgatory,
It locally contains, or heaven, or hell,
There's no third place in't.

  DUCH: How do you affect it?
  ANT: My banishment, feeding my melancholy,
Would often reason thus.
DUCH: Pray, let's hear it.
395 ANT: Say a man never marry, nor have children,
What takes that from him? only the bare name
Of being a father, or the weak delight
To see the little wanton ride a cock-horse
Upon a painted stick, or hear him chatter
400 Like a taught starling.

  DUCH: Fie, fie, what's all this?
One of your eyes is blood-shot; use my ring to't,
They say 'tis very sovereign: 'twas my wedding ring,
And I did vow never to part with it
But to my second husband.

405  ANT: You have parted with it now.
  DUCH: Yes, to help your eye-sight.
  ANT: You have made me stark blind.
  DUCH: How?
  ANT: There is a saucy and ambitious devil,
Is dancing in this circle.

  DUCH: Remove him.
  ANT: How?

DUCHESS: You mean my dead body, wrapped up in a sheet?
ANTONIO: I was thinking more like wrapped up in bedsheets...
DUCHESS: Gosh, that's a strange thing to put in a will!
ANTONIO: What would be strange is if you had no will to get married again.
DUCHESS: What's your opinion about marriage?
ANTONIO: I think of it like someone who doesn't believe in purgatory: marriage is either heaven or hell, there's no in-between.
DUCHESS: Which do you think it is?
ANTONIO: My loneliness, which can't help make me feel somewhat sad, makes me think of it like this —
DUCHESS: Please tell me.
ANTONIO: Imagine a man never gets married, nor has any children, what does he lose? Just the status of being a father, or the small delight of seeing his little child playing on a hobby horse, or of hearing the child chatter like a trained bird.

DUCHESS: Hey, hey, hey — what's all this? One of your eyes is weeping. Use my ring on it; they say it helps. It was my wedding ring, and I vowed never to part with it, except to give it to my next husband.

ANTONIO: But you've just given it to me.
DUCHESS: Yes, to help your eye.
ANTONIO: Instead, you've made me go completely blind.
DUCHESS: How?
ANTONIO: Blind with ambition. There is an immoral, ambitious devil dancing in this ring, tempting me with everything I want.
DUCHESS: Get him out of the way.
ANTONIO: How?

DUCH: There needs small conjuration, when your finger
410 May do it; thus; is it fit?

                                                                           [*He kneels.*]

ANT: What said you?
DUCH: Sir, this goodly roof of yours, is too low built;
I cannot stand upright in't nor discourse,
Without I raise it higher; raise yourself;
Or, if you please, my hand to help you: so.

415   ANT: Ambition, madam, is a great man's madness,
That is not kept in chains, and close-pent rooms,
But in fair lightsome lodgins, and is girt
With the wild noise of prattling visitants,
Which makes it lunatic beyond all cure.
420 Conceive not I am so stupid but I aim
Whereto your favours tend: but he's a fool,
That being a-cold, would thrust his hands i'th' fire
To warm them.
   DUCH: So now the ground's broke,
You may discover what a wealthy mine
425 I make you lord of.

   ANT: O, my unworthiness!
   DUCH: You were ill to sell yourself:
This darkening of your worth is not like that
Which tradesmen use i'th' city; their false lights
Are to rid bad wares off; and I must tell you,
430 If you will know where breathes a complete man,
(I speak it without flattery,) turn your eyes,
And progress through yourself.

   ANT: Were there nor heaven nor hell,
I should be honest: I have long serv'd virtue,
And ne'er ta'en wages of her.

   DUCH: Now she pays it.
435 The misery of us that are born great!

DUCHESS: You don't need any magic — just put your finger in the ring. Like this. Does it fit?

[*She puts the ring on his finger. He kneels.*]

ANTONIO: What did you say?

DUCHESS: Sir, this humility you're showing by kneeling is not comfortable. I can't talk to you on equal terms unless you stand back up. Get up or, if you want, let me help you up.

[*She raises him.*]

ANTONIO: Ambition, madam, corrupts great men, and it's not something that's safely contained, kept in chains or locked rooms; instead, ambition can lurk in the nicest places and nicest people, and is surrounded by the prattling noise of those people who chase after it, making it frenzied and Please don't think I am so stupid to attack you for your kindness, but I would be a fool to cause harm just to satisfy an ambitious desire.

DUCHESS: Now we've broken the ice and you're speaking more openly, I can show you how valuable my affection for you will be, and how it will make you a lord.

ANTONIO: Oh I am unworthy of you!

DUCHESS: You do wrong to demean yourself. Your obscuring of your own worth is not like the deception used by tradesmen in the city, who are deceitful to sell dodgy goods. I tell you, if you want to know where there is a complete, worthy man, and I say this without flattery, turn and look at yourself.

ANTONIO: Even if there were not the promise of heaven or the threat of hell, I still would've done by best to be a good man, and yet I've never gotten anything from it.

DUCHESS: Now's your chance. Ah. the misery of us high-status people!

We are forc'd to woo, because none dare woo us;
And as a tyrant doubles with his words,
And fearfully equivocates, so we
Are forc'd to express our violent passions
440 In riddles, and in dreams, and leave the path
Of simple virtue, which was never made
To seem the thing it is not. Go, go brag
You have left me heartless; mine is in your bosom:
I hope 'twill multiply love there. You do tremble:
445 Make not your heart so dead a piece of flesh,
To fear, more than to love me. Sir, be confident:
What is't distracts you? This is flesh and blood sir;
'Tis not the figure cut in alabaster,
Kneels at my husbands tomb. Awake, awake, man!
450 I do here put off all vain ceremony,
And only do appear to you a young widow
That claims you for her husband, and like a widow,
I use but half a blush in't.
   ANT: Truth speak for me:
I will remain the constant sanctuary
455 Of your good name.
   DUCH: I thank you, gentle love:
and 'cause you shall not come to me in debt,
Being now my steward, here upon your lips
I sign your Quietus est. This you should have begg'd now;
I have seen children oft eat sweetmeats thus,
460 As fearful to devour them too soon.

   ANT: But for your brothers?
   DUCH: Do not think of them:
All discord without this circumference
Is only to be pitied, and not fear'd:
Yet, should they know it, time will easily
465 Scatter the tempest.
   ANT: These words should be mine,
And all the parts you have spoke, if some part of it
Would not have savour'd flattery.
   DUCH: Kneel.

We have to do all the chasing when it comes to romance, because others are too scared to chase us! Just as a tyrant is deceptive with his words, we too have to speak in riddles and dreams to show our feelings for someone, and that means we sacrifice our goodness because it's not good to try and hide how we feel. Go, go boast to your mates how you've left me heartless, because my heart is now in you – I hope it will grow more love in there. You're shaking: don't let your heart become so lifeless that you fear me more than you love me. Sir, be honest, what it is that makes you hesitate? This, my body, is flesh and blood, not the stone of the statue of me that was carved and placed in my first husband's tomb. Pull yourself together man!
I'm being completely open and honest with you here, and stand before you as nothing more than a young widow who wants you to be her husband. And I'm not ashamed of it.

ANTONIO: Truth speaks for me: I must not do anything to harm your reputation.

DUCHESS: Thank you, gentle love, and because I don't want you to be in my debt, I will show with this kiss that our accounts are settled and we are on equal terms. You should have been begging for that. You're like a child who puts off eating a sweet because they don't want the enjoyment to be over.
ANTONIO: Shouldn't we be worried about your brothers?
DUCHESS: Nah. Any problems outside our own circle are just to be pitied, not worried about. And even if they do find out, they'll get over it with time.

ANTONIO: It should have been me to say such reassuring things, and everything else you've said, if only you hadn't said them so well yourself.
DUCHESS: Get on your knees.

[*Enter* CARIOLA.]

ANT: Ha!

DUCH: Be not amaz'd, this woman's of my counsel:
I have heard lawyers say, a contract in a chamber
470 Per verba presenti is absolute marriage.
Bless, heaven, this sacred gordian, which let violence
Never untwine!

ANT: And may our sweet affections, like the spheres,
Be still in motion.

DUCH: Quickening, and make
The like soft music.

475 ANT: That we may imitate the loving palms,
Best emblem of a peaceful marriage
That never bore fruit divided.

DUCH: What can the church force more?

ANT: That fortune may not know an accident
480 Either of joy, or sorrow, to divide
Our fixed wishes.

DUCH: How can the church build faster?
We now are man and wife, and 'tis the church
That must but echo this. Maid, stand apart:
485 I now am blind.

ANT: What's your conceit in this?

DUCH: I would have you lead your fortune by the hand
Unto your marriage bed:
(You speak in me this, for we now are one:)
We'll only lie, and talk together, and plot
490 T'appease my humourous kindred; and if you please,
Like the old tale in Alexander and Lodowick,
Lay a naked sword between us, keep us chaste.
O, let me shroud my blushes in your bosom,
Since 'tis the treasury of all my secrets!

[*Exeunt.*]

[*Enter* CARIOLA.]

ANTONIO: Oh my God!

DUCHESS: Don't be startled; this woman is someone I trust, and she is here to serve as witness at our wedding and therefore make it official. May heaven bless this sacred knot of our union, which no violence will be able to untie.

ANTONIO: And may our love for one another move like the heavenly bodies.

DUCHESS: Growing, shining, coming to life, and making soft music.

ANTONIO: We will be like the two palm trees that lean toward one another and are known as a symbol for the perfect marriage, and that never grow fruit when separated.

DUCHESS: What else could the Church want to enforce?

ANTONIO: That fate has nothing in store for us, either something happy or sad, that could separate us.

DUCHESS: How could the Church build a more secure union between us? We are man and wife, and the Church only has to agree. Cariola, move aside. I am now blind.

ANTONIO: What are you playing at?

DUCHESS: I need you to hold my hand and lead me to bed, which is your wish too; I know, because we're now one. We'll just lie together, talk, think of ways to keep my brothers happy, and if you want, we can follow the old custom of laying a sword between us (to stop us having sex). Oh let me hide my blushes against your chest, since it is where all my secrets are now kept!

[*They exit.*]

495 CARI: Whether the spirit of greatness, or of woman
Reign most in her, I know not; but it shews
A fearful madness: I owe her much of pity.

[*Exit.*]

### WHAT'S GOING ON?

*With an immediate slap-in-the-face to her brothers' instructions, the Duchess secretly marries her servant Antonio. They clearly love each other in a deeper way than mere lust – she speaks about his goodness, his merit as a person, and Antonio's comments to Delio earlier established his sincere devotion to her. But Antonio is concerned about being guilty of ambition – in marrying the Duchess, he is also elevating*

## ORIGINAL — ACT TWO

CARIOLA: I'm not whether the Duchess has been led by a rational wisdom or an irrational passion, but it seems like madness. I feel very sorry for her.

*[Exit.]*

*his own social position. This means the Duchess, to her frustration, has to play the dominant role in their (quite quick) courtship.*

*It's easy to see the Duchess's actions as heroically subversive in her oppressive patriarchal environment, but Cariola raises a pertinent question at the end — is the Duchess in fact guilty of acting according to the archaic misogynistic stereotype of women being driven by passion rather than logic?*

ACT TWO

Scene One

[*Enter* BOSOLA *and* CAST:.]

BOS: You say you would fain be taken for an eminent courtier?
CAST: 'Tis the very main of my ambition.
BOS: Let me see: you have a reasonable good face for 't already, and your night-cap expresses your ears sufficient largely. I would have you learn to twirl the strings of your band with a good grace, and in a set speech, at th' end of every sentence, to hum three or four times, or blow your nose till it smart again, to recover your memory. When you come to be a president in criminal causes, if you smile upon a prisoner, hang him; but if you frown upon him and threaten him, let him be sure to scape the gallows.
CAST: I would be a very merry president.
BOS: Do not sup o' nights; 'twill beget you an admirable wit.
CAST: Rather it would make me have a good stomach to quarrel; for they say, your roaring boys eat meat seldom, and that makes them so valiant. But how shall I know whether the people take me for an eminent fellow?
BOS: I will teach a trick to know it: give out you lie a-dying, and if you hear the common people curse you, be sure you are taken for one of the prime night-caps.

[*Enter an* OLD LADY]

You come from painting now.
OLD LADY. From what?

SCENE ONE        MODERN

[*Enter* BOSOLA  CASTRUCHIO — *the court at Malfi.*]

BOSOLA: You say you want to be a high-ranking courtier?

CASTRUCHIO: It is my greatest ambition.
BOSOLA: Well, you have the right sort of face for it, and your hat makes your ears look sufficiently large. You should learn to fiddle elegantly with the strings in your collar, and when giving a speech, finish every sentence by humming, or by blowing your nose until it hurts, to help remember the next lines you've rehearsed. When you're in charge of a criminal lawsuit, smile at the prisoners you intend to hang and threaten the ones you intend to set free.

CASTRUCHIO: I'd be a jolly judge.
BOSOLA: Do not eat your dinner late at night, as it will sharpen your intelligence too much.
CASTRUCHIO: Instead, it will make me have an appetite for a fight, as they say rowdy young men rarely eat meat, and that's what makes them so bold. But how will I know the people take me seriously?
BOSOLA: I'll teach you a trick: if they hear you're dying, and they curse you, then you'll know you're taken for a true lawyer. [Webster does some odd conflating of "courtier" and "lawyer" in this section; they were not the same thing.]

[*Enter* OLD LADY.]

You've just come from doing your painting.
OLD LADY: From what?

BOS: Why, from your scurvy face-physic. To behold
thee not painted inclines somewhat near a miracle.
These in thy face here were deep ruts and foul sloughs
the last progress. There was a lady in France that, having
had the small-pox, flayed the skin off her face to make it
more level; and whereas before she looked like a nutmeg-
grater, after she resembled an abortive hedge-hog.

OLD LADY. Do you call this painting?
BOS: No, no, but you call [it] careening of an old
morphewed lady,
to make her disembogue again: there's rough-cast phrase
to your plastic.
OLD LADY. It seems you are well acquainted with my
closet.
BOS: One would suspect it for a shop of witchcraft, to
find in it the fat of serpents, spawn of snakes, Jews'
spittle, and their young children's ordure; and all these
for the face. I would sooner eat a dead pigeon taken from
the soles of the feet of one sick of the plague, than kiss
one of you fasting. Here are two of you, whose sin of
your youth is the very patrimony of the physician; makes
him renew his foot-cloth with the spring, and change his
high-pric'd courtezan with the fall of the leaf. I do
wonder you do not loathe yourselves. Observe my
meditation now.
What thing is in this outward form of man
To be belov'd? We account it ominous,
If nature do produce a colt, or lamb,
A fawn, or goat, in any limb resembling
A man, and fly from 't as a prodigy:
Man stands amaz'd to see his deformity
In any other creature but himself.
But in our own flesh though we bear diseases
Which have their true names only ta'en from beasts,—
As the most ulcerous wolf and swinish measle,—

## SCENE ONE — MODERN

BOSOLA: From treating your scurvy face with makeup. It's blatantly obvious — your face is plastered in it. To think you weren't painted would require a miracle.
I can still see the deep ruts and foul ditches in your face you've tried to cover up. There was a lady in France who, after having had small pox, scraped the skin off her face to make it more level. Before, the small pox made her skin look like a nutmeg grater, and after, she looked like an aborted hedgehog.
OLD LADY: You're calling my makeup "painting"?
BOSOLA: No, no, but you could call it scraping off the barnacles from a ship's hull so it can be filled with sailors, ready for the sea. Those are some words for you that are as rough as your face.
OLD LADY: It seems you have a good knowledge of my closet [where she does her makeup].

BOSOLA: One would imagine it's like a shop of witchcraft, full of fat serpents and snakes' babies, the spit of Jews and their children's faeces — and all of this for your face. I would rather eat a dead pigeon taken from the soles of the feet of someone with the plague than kiss someone like you. Look at the pair of you, with your sexually transmitted diseases that keep your doctors rich; you must have to pay them so much that they can by new shoes and new prostitutes whenever they fancy. I wonder why you don't both despise yourselves. Listen to me now.

Why are people obsessed with their outward appearance? We find it sinister when an animal, by freak of nature, looks like a person, and run away from it as something supernatural. People are horrified to see their own form in all things but themselves.

But though our flesh is full of disgusting diseases that are named after animals,

ORIGINAL                    ACT TWO

    Though we are eaten up of lice and worms,
    And though continually we bear about us
60  A rotten and dead body, we delight
    To hide it in rich tissue: all our fear,
    Nay, all our terror, is, lest our physician
    Should put us in the ground to be made sweet.—
    Your wife 's gone to Rome: you two couple, and get you
65  to the wells at Lucca to recover your aches. I have other
    work on foot.      [*Exeunt* CAST: *and* OLD LADY]

### WHAT'S GOING ON?
*Many productions skip this opening to the scene, because it delays the plot – but it's good for seeing Bosola fitting very well into the bitter malcontent archetype.*

  BOS: I observe our duchess
Is sick a-days, she pukes, her stomack seethes,
The fins of her eye-lids look most teeming blue,
She wanes i' the cheek, and waxes fat i' the flank,
70  And, contrary to our Italian fashion,
Wears a loose-bodied gown: there 's somewhat in 't.
I have a trick may chance discover it,
A pretty one; I have bought some apricocks,
The first our spring yields.

      [*Enter* ANTONIO *and* DELIO, *talking together apart.*]

  DEL:    And so long since married?
You amaze me.
75  ANT:    Let me seal your lips for ever:
For, did I think that anything but th' air
Could carry these words from you, I should wish
You had no breath at all.—Now, sir, in your contemplation?
You are studying to become a great wise fellow.

SCENE ONE　　　　　　MODERN

though we are corrupt, as if full of lice and worms,
and though we always carry our corrupt bodies around with
us, we delight to hide it all in elegant clothing. And yet our
greatest fear is that our doctors will send us to the grave,
where we'll become food for the same worms that rot us on
the inside.
Both of you should get together, now your wife's gone to
Rome, Castruchio, and go to the baths at Lucca to ease your
venereal sickness. I've got work to do.

[*Exeunt* CASTRUCHIO *and* OLD LADY.]

*His misogyny is firmly established, as is his contempt toward the human condition, which he sees as being inherently corrupt.*

BOSOLA: I've been watching the Duchess and have noticed
she's feeling sick. She pukes, her stomach's hurting, and the
edges of her eyelids look very blue, as pregnant women's
are. She's growing thin in the cheek, and getting fat around
the hips. And she goes against our normal fashion by
wearing a loose-fitting gown...it's not just a coincidence. I
have a trick to expose it, and an appealing one. I have
some lovely fresh apricots [thought to induce labour].

[*Enter* ANTONIO *and* DELIO:]

DELIO: And it's been so long since you got married? I'm
astonished.
ANTONIO: You've got to keep your lips sealed. I'd rather
you were dead rather than you tell anyone about this. Ah,
Bosola – what are you thinking about? I guess you're
thinking about how to become a great wise fellow.

80  BOS: O, sir, the opinion of wisdom is a foul tetter that
runs all over a man's body: if simplicity direct us to have
no evil, it directs us to a happy being; for the subtlest
folly proceeds from the subtlest wisdom: let me be simply
honest.
85  ANT: I do understand your inside.
BOS:     Do you so?
ANT: Because you would not seem to appear to th'
world
Puff'd up with your preferment, you continue
This out-of-fashion melancholy: leave it, leave it.
90  BOS: Give me leave to be honest in any phrase, in any
compliment whatsoever. Shall I confess myself to you? I
look no higher than I can reach: they are the gods that
must ride on winged horses. A lawyer's mule of a slow
pace will both suit my disposition and business; for, mark
95  me, when a man's mind rides faster than his horse can
gallop, they quickly both tire.

ANT: You would look up to heaven, but I think
The devil, that rules i' th' air, stands in your light.
BOS: O, sir, you are lord of the ascendant, chief man
100  with the duchess: a duke was your cousin-german
remov'd. Say you were lineally descended from King
Pepin, or he himself, what of this? Search the heads of
the greatest rivers in the world, you shall find them but
bubbles of water. Some would think the souls of princes
105  were brought forth by some more weighty cause than
those of meaner persons: they are deceiv'd, there's the
same hand to them; the like passions sway them; the
same reason that makes a vicar go to law for a tithe-pig,
and undo his neighbours, makes them spoil a whole
110  province, and batter down goodly cities with the cannon.

[*Enter* DUCHESS *and* Ladies]

DUCH: Your arm, Antonio: do I not grow fat?

SCENE ONE     MODERN

BOSOLA: Bah; I think wisdom is like a disease than runs over a man's body. Being simple-minded means being too stupid to be evil, and therefore is the way to being happy. So being foolish is a kind of wisdom, if I'm being honest.

ANTONIO: I know why you say things like this.

BOSOLA: Oh do you?

ANTONIO: You don't want to seem as if your promotion to the Duchess's stableman has made you arrogant, so you keep acting all miserable. Stop it, stop it.

BOSOLA: Give me permission to be completely honest. Shall I tell you the truth about me? I am not ambitious; ambitious people are like fake gods who can't actually get up to heaven and need a flying horse to carry them. So unambitious am I, that all I need is a ploddy mule like lawyers use. Hear my words: if a man desires things that his capabilities won't allow him to achieve, he'll come to a bad end.

ANTONIO: You want to be ambitious, but I think something evil is blocking your way.

BOSOLA: Oh, sir, you are the person of highest influence, the Duchess's chief man: a duke was your first cousin. Imagine you were descended from the ruler of the Roman empire, what would that matter? Great rivers come from the same source as lesser rivers, just as great people come from the same place as other people. Some people think princes were created by more important forces than normal people, but it's not true; we were all shaped by the same hand, and we think with the same logic that makes a Catholic vicar ruin his neighbours over a debt and makes them destroy whole provinces and cities out of revenge.

[*Enter* DUCHESS *and* Ladies.]

DUCHESS: Let me hold your arm, Antonio. Do you think I'm getting fat?

51

I am exceeding short-winded.—Bosola,
I would have you, sir, provide for me a litter;
Such a one as the Duchess of Florence rode in.
   BOS: The duchess us'd one when she was great with
child.
   DUCH: I think she did.—Come hither, mend my ruff:
Here, when? thou art such a tedious lady; and
Thy breath smells of lemon-pills: would thou hadst done!
Shall I swoon under thy fingers? I am
So troubled with the mother!

   BOS:    *[Aside]* I fear too much.
   DUCH: I have heard you say that the French courtiers
Wear their hats on 'fore that king.

   ANT: I have seen it.
   DUCH:    In the presence?
   ANT:    Yes.
   DUCH: Why should not we bring up that fashion?
'Tis ceremony more than duty that consists
In the removing of a piece of felt.
Be you the example to the rest o' th' court;
Put on your hat first.
   ANT:    You must pardon me:
I have seen, in colder countries than in France,
Nobles stand bare to th' prince; and the distinction
Methought show'd reverently.
   BOS: I have a present for your grace.
   DUCH:    For me, sir?
   BOS: Apricocks, madam.
   DUCH:    O, sir, where are they?
I have heard of none to-year

   BOS:    *[Aside]* Good; her colour rises.
   DUCH: Indeed, I thank you: they are wondrous fair
ones.
What an unskilful fellow is our gardener!
We shall have none this month.

SCENE ONE         MODERN

I'm really out of breath. Bosola, I want you to
fetch me a litter [curtained bed/chair carried by servants]
like the one the Duchess of Florence rode in.
BOSOLA: That Duchess used a litter when she was pregnant.

DUCHESS: I think she did. [To servant] Come here, straighten
out my collar: Hurry up; you're such a slow lady, and your
breath smells of lemon peel. Do hurry up [as the woman
fusses with the Duchess's collar] or I'll faint under your
fingers! I'm feeling hysterical, like a mother! ["Troubled with
the mother" would mean feeling hysterical, but of course
Bosola senses the other meaning.]
BOSOLA: [Aside] I suspect very much like a mother.
DUCHESS: I've heard you say that French courtiers wear
their hats in the presence of their king.
ANTONIO: It's true; I've seen it.
DUCHESS: Truly, when they're in the presence of the king?
ANTONIO: Yes.
DUCHESS: Why shouldn't we start that fashion? It's just a
meaningless ceremony to remove a hat. Be the example
that starts the trend: put on your hat right now.


ANTONIO: You must pardon me for not putting on my hat,
but I've seen, in colder countries than France, nobles
standing without a hat in front of the prince, which I thought
showed their respect.

BOSOLA: I have a present for your Grace.
DUCHESS: For me?
BOSOLA: Apricots, madam.

DUCHESS: Oh, where did you get them from? I heard there
weren't any this year.
BOSOLA: [Aside] As I suspected: her skin's reddening, as a
pregnant person's does.
DUCHESS: I thank you: they are delicious. What an idiot our
gardener is!
We'll have no apricots this month.

53

BOS: Will not your grace pare them?

DUCH: No: they taste of musk, methinks; indeed they do.

140 BOS: I know not: yet I wish your grace had par'd 'em.

DUCH: Why?
BOS: I forgot to tell you, the knave gardener,
Only to raise his profit by them the sooner,
Did ripen them in horse-dung.
DUCH: O, you jest.—
You shall judge: pray, taste one.
145 ANT: Indeed, madam,
I do not love the fruit.
DUCH: Sir, you are loth
To rob us of our dainties. 'Tis a delicate fruit;
They say they are restorative.
BOS: 'Tis a pretty art,
This grafting.
DUCH: 'Tis so; a bettering of nature.
150 BOS: To make a pippin grow upon a crab,
A damson on a black-thorn.—*[Aside]* How greedily she eats them!
A whirlwind strike off these bawd farthingales!
For, but for that and the loose-bodied gown,
I should have discover'd apparently
155 The young springal cutting a caper in her belly.
DUCH: I thank you, Bosola: they were right good ones,
If they do not make me sick.
ANT: How now, madam!
DUCH: This green fruit and my stomach are not friends:
How they swell me!
160 BOS: *[Aside]* Nay, you are too much swell'd already.
DUCH: O, I am in an extreme cold sweat!
BOS: I am very sorry. [*Exit.*]

SCENE ONE           MODERN

BOSOLA: Aren't you going to take the skin off them, your Grace?

DUCHESS: No, they taste nice as they are.

BOSOLA: I wouldn't know, but I do wish you'd taken the skin off.

DUCHESS: Why?

BOSOLA: I forgot to tell you: the scoundrel gardener, to save some money, used horse-dung as fertiliser, so they might still have some horse poo on them.

DUCHESS: Oh, you're joking...Antonio, you test it for horse dung.

ANTONIO: No thanks; I'm not a fan of apricots.

DUCHESS: Sir, you're just being kind and saving them for me. People say apricots are good for your health.

BOSOLA: It's an impressive art, this grafting, mixing one species of plant with another, which is used to farm apricots.

DUCHESS: Yes; it's an improvement of nature's own way.

BOSOLA: To make a pippin apple grow on a crab-apple tree, or a damson on a blackthorn. [Aside] How greedily she eats them! If it weren't for the farthingales [hoops used to make a skirt stand out widely, as was fashionable], I suspect I'd see her pregnant belly pressed against her dress with the infant dancing inside it.

DUCHESS: Thanks Bosola; those apricots were terrific — except they've made me feel sick.

ANTONIO: What?!

DUCHESS: This green fruit and my stomach do not mix well — they've made my belly swollen!

BOSOLA: [Aside] No, your belly was already much too swollen.

DUCHESS: Oh, I'm feeling awful!

BOSOLA: I am so sorry. [Exit.]

ORIGINAL                    ACT TWO

DUCH: Lights to my chamber!—O good Antonio,
I fear I am undone!

DEL: Lights there, lights! [*Exeunt* DUCHESS *and*
Ladies.]

ANT: O my most trusty Delio, we are lost!
165 I fear she 's fall'n in labour; and there 's left
No time for her remove.

DEL:      Have you prepar'd
Those ladies to attend to her; and procur'd
That politic safe conveyance for the midwife
Your duchess plotted?

ANT:      I have.

170 DEL: Make use, then, of this forc'd occasion.
Give out that Bosola hath poison'd her
With these apricocks; that will give some colour
For her keeping close.

ANT:      Fie, fie, the physicians
Will then flock to her.

DEL: For that you may pretend
175 She 'll use some prepar'd antidote of her own,
Lest the physicians should re-poison her.

ANT: I am lost in amazement: I know not what to
think on 't.                                    [*Exeunt.*]

### WHAT'S GOING ON?

*Bosola fulfils his new job of being a spy quite efficiently — the Duchess is in great danger of having her secret pregnancy exposed to the public. But the ridiculous way he goes about it — with apparently supercharged apricots — prevents him from coming across as a Machiavellian genius. Webster's original script changes "apricots" to "apricocks",*

SCENE ONE                    MODERN

DUCHESS: Light the way to my bedroom! Oh, Antonio, I fear I'm ruined! [*Exit.*]
DELIO: Hey, servants, get some lights!

ANTONIO: Oh my trusted Delio, we're doomed! I fear she's in labour, and there's no time to whisk her away so the baby can be born in secret.

DELIO: Have you prepared trustworthy maids to help her? And cunningly arranged for the midwife your Duchess wanted to help her?

ANTONIO: I have.

DELIO: Then work this situation to your advantage. Spread the rumour that Bosola has poisoned her with these apricots — everyone knows he's a criminal, and it will give some justification for keeping the Duchess hidden safely away.
ANTONIO: No, no, the doctors will then want to flock around her.
DELIO: Then tell them she will use her own medicine, to prevent any untrustworthy doctor giving her more poison.

ANTONIO: This utterly bewildering. I haven't a clue how to handle all this.                          [*Exeunt.*]

---

*and this scene is an important demonstration of an invasive male authority over the female body. It also builds on the Duchess's blithe naivety, seen in the previous act — despite wanting to keep her marriage and pregnancy secret from the world, she doesn't do a great job of hiding it here; there's a lot of physical contact with Antonio and she allows her appetite to guide her behaviour rather than cautious logic.*

---

Scene Two

[*Enter* BOSOLA *and* Old Lady.]

BOS: So, so, there's no question but her techiness and most vulturous eating of the apricocks are apparent signs of breeding, now?
OLD LADY. I am in haste, sir.
BOS: There was a young waiting-woman had a monstrous desire to see the glass-house—
OLD LADY. Nay, pray, let me go.
BOS: And it was only to know what strange instrument it was should swell up a glass to the fashion of a woman's belly.

OLD LADY. I will hear no more of the glass-house. You are still abusing women!
BOS: Who, I? No; only, by the way now and then, mention your frailties. The orange-tree bears ripe and green fruit and blossoms all together; and some of you give entertainment for pure love, but more for more precious reward. The lusty spring smells well; but drooping autumn tastes well. If we have the same golden showers that rained in the time of Jupiter the thunderer, you have the same Danaës still, to hold up their laps to receive them. Didst thou never study the mathematics?

OLD LADY. What's that, sir?
BOS: Why, to know the trick how to make a many lines meet in one centre.

SCENE TWO          MODERN

[*Enter* BOSOLA *and* OLD LADY.]

BOSOLA: So, there's no doubt that her irritability and ravenous eating of the apricots are obvious signs of her being pregnant, right?
OLD LADY: I'm in a hurry, sir.
BOSOLA: There's a story of a young maid who had a desperate desire to see the glass-factory —
OLD LADY: No, don't tell me your story, just let me go.
BOSOLA: And she only wanted to see it in order to know what strange instrument would swell up glass to the shape of a woman's belly. ["Instrument" would have been taken as innuendo for male genitalia, so this story is another misogynistic gybe by Bosola].
OLD LADY: I don't want to hear any more about the glass-factory. You're still being a sexist pig!
BOSOLA: Who, me? No, all I do is make occasional mention of women's weaknesses. All women, whether they are young, like orange-tree blossom, or middle aged, like its green fruit, or old, like its ripe oranges, are lustful. Some of you like sex purely for the enjoyment, but most women expect some sort of payment out of it. The lusty younger women are attractive for their beauty, but older, more experienced women in their autumn years are more rewarding to have sex with. Even today, young women still eagerly expect a reward for sex. (Bosola's deeply distasteful analogy refers to the golden shower of rain by which Jupiter impregnated Danaes, and by this implies young women want "gold"/a payment for sex.] Did you never study mathematics?
OLD LADY: What do you mean?
BOSOLA: To learn the trick for making many lines [innuendo for male genitalia] meet in one centre [female genitalia].

59

25  Go, go, give your foster-daughters good counsel: tell them, that the devil takes delight to hang at a woman's girdle, like a false rusty watch, that she cannot discern how the time passes.

*[Exit Old Lady.]*
*[Enter ANTONIO, RODERIGO, and GRISOLAN.]*

ANT: Shut up the court-gates.
ROD. Why sir? What's the danger?
ANT: Shut up the posterns presently, and call
All the officers o' th' court.
30  GRIS. I shall instantly. *[Exit.]*
ANT: Who keeps the key o' th' park-gate?
ROD. Forobosco.
ANT: Let him bring 't presently.

*[Re-enter GRISOLAN with Servants]*
FIRST SERV. O, gentleman o' th' court, the foulest treason!
BOS: [aside.] If that these apricocks should be poison'd now,
Without my knowledge?
35  FIRST SERV. There was taken even now a Switzer in the duchess' bed-chamber—
SECOND SERV. A Switzer!
FIRST SERV. With a pistol in his great codpiece.
BOS: Ha, ha, ha!
FIRST SERV. The codpiece was the case for 't.

SECOND SERV. There was a cunning traitor. Who would have search'd his codpiece?
40  FIRST SERV. True; if he had kept out of the ladies' chambers. And all the moulds of his buttons were leaden bullets.
SECOND SERV. O wicked cannibal! A fire-lock in 's codpiece!
FIRST SERV. 'Twas a French plot, upon my life.

SCENE TWO                MODERN

Go away; go and give your foster daughters some good advice: tell them that the devil hangs at a woman's waist, making them so fixated on their immoral lust that they forget what's going on around them.

> [*Exit* OLD LADY.]
> [*Enter* ANTONIO, RODERIGO *and* GRISOLAN.]

ANTONIO: Lock up the court gates.
RODERIGO: Why?

ANTONIO: Lock up the back gates immediately, and gather all the servants of the court.
GRISOLAN: I'll get right on it. [*Exit.*]

ANTONIO: Who's got the key to the garden gates?
RODERIGO: Forobosco has it.
ANTONIO: Tell him to bring it immediately.

> [*Re-enter* GRISOLAN *with* Servants.]

FIRST SERVANT: Oh, gentlemen of the court, the foulest treason against the Duchess has occurred!
BOSOLA: [*Aside*] Uh oh — what if those apricots I gave to her had been poisoned without me knowing about it…?

FIRST SERVANT: Just now a Swiss soldier was seen in the Duchess's bedroom —
SECOND SERVANT: A Swiss soldier?!

FIRST SERVANT: With a pistol in his huge codpiece.
BOSOLA: Ha, ha, ha!
FIRST SERVANT: The codpiece was where he kept the gun hidden.
SECOND SERVANT: Then he was a clever traitor, because who'd want to search a codpiece?
FIRST SERVANT: True; well, he would have been clever if he'd kept out of the ladies' bedrooms. And all the buttons on his clothes were actually bullets.
SECOND SERVANT: What a wicked savage! A gun in his codpiece!
FIRST SERVANT: It was a French plot to kill the Duchess, I swear on my life it was.

ORIGINAL                              ACT TWO

SECOND SERV. To see what the devil can do!

ANT: Are all the officers here?
SERVANTS. We are.
ANT: Gentlemen,
45 We have lost much plate, you know; and but this evening
Jewels, to the value of four thousand ducats,
Are missing in the duchess' cabinet.
Are the gates shut?
SERV.     Yes.
ANT:      'Tis the duchess' pleasure
Each officer be lock'd into his chamber
50 Till the sun-rising; and to send the keys
Of all their chests and of their outward doors
Into her bed-chamber. She is very sick.
ROD. At her pleasure.
ANT: She entreats you take 't not ill: the innocent
55 Shall be the more approv'd by it.
BOS: Gentlemen o' the wood-yard, where 's your Switzer now?
FIRST SERV. By this hand, 'twas credibly reported by one o' the black guard. [*Exeunt all except* ANTONIO *and* DELIO.]

---

### WHAT'S GOING ON?

*Antonio does his best to keep control in the spiralling chaos. The rumour of a random Swiss guy raiding the Duchess's palace seems crazy, but it shows the power of rumour/gossip in this world, especially as it's not clear who started it. Antonio starts a rumour of his own — that the Duchess's jewels have been stolen, and everyone*

---

DELIO. How fares it with the duchess?
ANT:    She 's expos'd
60 Unto the worst of torture, pain, and fear.
DELIO. Speak to her all happy comfort.

SCENE TWO                    MODERN

SECOND SERVANT: It's amazing to see what evil the devil is capable of!
ANTONIO: Are all the servants here?
SERVANTS: We are.
ANTONIO: Gentlemen, we have lost a lot of our silverware, and a lot of jewels, all to the value of four thousand ducats, gone missing from the Duchess's rooms. Are the gates shut?

SERVANT: Yes.
ANTONIO: It is the Duchess's will that each servant be locked in his bedroom until dawn, and to send the keys for all their chests and doors to her bedroom. She is very concerned.

RODERIGO: Whatever she wants.
ANTONIO: She asks you not to be offended: the innocent among you will be all the more praised.
BOSOLA: You lowly woodcutters, where's your supposed Swiss soldier now?
FIRST SERVANT: I swear, it was reliably reported by one of the kitchen servants.

[*Exeunt all except* ANTONIO *and* DELIO.]

*needs to be locked up until the culprit is found. This is a cover story just to keep prying eyes away from the Duchess while she gives birth.*
*Does Antonio's deception sink him down to Bosola's moral level? Or does his more benign motivation for being deceptive mean we don't condemn him so much as Bosola?*

DELIO: How's the Duchess doing?
ANTONIO: She's vulnerable to the worst of torture, pain and fear.
DELIO: Reassure her as best you can.

ANT: How I do play the fool with mine own danger!
You are this night, dear friend, to post to Rome:
My life lies in your service.
DELIO.     Do not doubt me.
ANT: O, 'tis far from me: and yet fear presents me
Somewhat that looks like danger.
DELIO.     Believe it,
'Tis but the shadow of your fear, no more:
How superstitiously we mind our evils!
The throwing down salt, or crossing of a hare,
Bleeding at nose, the stumbling of a horse,
Or singing of a cricket, are of power
To daunt whole man in us. Sir, fare you well:
I wish you all the joys of a bless'd father;
And, for my faith, lay this unto your breast,—
Old friends, like old swords, still are trusted best. [*Exit.*]

[*Enter* CARIOLA]

CARI: Sir, you are the happy father of a son:
Your wife commends him to you.
ANT:     Blessèd comfort!—
For heaven's sake, tend her well; I'll presently
Go set a figure for 's nativity.

[*Exeunt.*]

SCENE TWO  MODERN

ANTONIO: How I'm foolishly risking my own safety! My dear friend, tonight you must ride quickly to Rome: my life depends on your help.

DELIO: You can rely on me.

ANTONIO: I know. And yet my fear is making me see something dangerous approaching.

DELIO: Believe it is nothing more than a projection of your fear. How superstitious we are! Such innocent. simple things like dropping salt, or a hare crossing our path, or a nosebleed, or a horse stumbling, or a cricket singing have the power to utterly terrify people, because they're taken as signs of terrible things. Sir, fare well, I wish you all the joys of a happy father; and, to remind you of my loyalty, remember this: old friends, just like old swords, are the most reliable.

[*Exit* DELIO.]

[*Enter* CARIOLA.]

CARIOLA: Sir, your son has just been born. Your wife entrusts you with him.

ANTONIO: Oh, wonderful! For heaven's sake, look after her. I'll immediately go and get a horoscope written for the baby.

[*Exeunt.*]

## Scene Three

[Enter BOSOLA, with a dark lantern]

BOS: Sure I did hear a woman shriek: list, ha!
And the sound came, if I receiv'd to right,
From the duchess' lodgings. There 's some stratagem
In the confining all our courtiers
5   To their several wards: I must have part of it;
My intelligence will freeze else. List, again!
It may be 'twas the melancholy bird,
Best friend of silence and of solitariness,
The owl, that screamed so.—Ha! Antonio!

[*Enter ANTONIO with a candle, his sword drawn*]

ANT: I heard some noise.—Who 's there? What art
10  thou? Speak.
BOS: Antonio, put not your face nor body
To such a forc'd expression of fear;
I am Bosola, your friend.
ANT:       Bosola!—
[*Aside*] This mole does undermine me.—Heard you not
A noise even now?

BOS:       From whence?
15  ANT:       From the duchess' lodging.
BOS: Not I: did you?
ANT:       I did, or else I dream'd.
BOS: Let 's walk towards it.
ANT:       No: it may be 'twas
But the rising of the wind.
BOS:       Very likely.

SCENE THREE        MODERN

[*Enter* BOSOLA, with a dark lantern.]

BOSOLA: I could've sworn I heard a woman shriek – yes! Again! The sound came, if I heard right, from the Duchess's lodgings. There's some scheme afoot, some deeper plan beneath shutting all the courtiers in their rooms. I must find out what it is, or I won't be much of a spy. There's the noise again! Perhaps it was just the melancholy owl, the best friend of silence and loneliness, that screamed. Ah! Antonio!

[*Enter* ANTONIO *with a candle and his sword drawn.*]

ANTONIO: I heard a noise – who's there? Who are you? Speak.
BOSOLA: Antonio, don't be so frightened; I am Bosola, your friend.

ANTONIO: Bosola! [*Aside*] This man is like a spy who seeks to deceive me. [NB. Antonio does not know that Bosola has been employed as a spy by Ferdinand.] Did you hear that noise just now?
BOSOLA: From where?

ANTONIO: From the Duchess's rooms.
BOSOLA: No I didn't. Did you?
ANTONIO: I did, unless I imagined it.
BOSOLA: Let's investigate it.
ANTONIO: No – it was probably just a gust of wind.
BOSOLA: Quite probably.

Methinks 'tis very cold, and yet you sweat:
You look wildly.
20   ANT:     I have been setting a figure
For the duchess' jewels.
   BOS:     Ah, and how falls your question?
Do you find it radical?
   ANT:     What's that to you?
'Tis rather to be question'd what design,
When all men were commanded to their lodgings,
Makes you a night-walker.
25   BOS:     In sooth, I'll tell you:
Now all the court's asleep, I thought the devil
Had least to do here; I came to say my prayers;
And if it do offend you I do so,
You are a fine courtier.
   ANT:     [*Aside*] This fellow will undo me.—
30   You gave the duchess apricocks to-day:
Pray heaven they were not poison'd!
   BOS: Poison'd! A Spanish fig
For the imputation!
   ANT:     Traitors are ever confident
Till they are discover'd. There were jewels stol'n too:
In my conceit, none are to be suspected
More than yourself.
35   BOS:     You are a false steward.
   ANT: Saucy slave, I'll pull thee up by the roots.
   BOS: May be the ruin will crush you to pieces.
   ANT: You are an impudent snake indeed, sir:
Are you scarce warm, and do you show your sting?

   BOS: ...
   ANT: You libel well, sir?
40   BOS:     No, sir: copy it out,
And I will set my hand to 't.
   ANT:     [Aside.] My nose bleeds.
One that were superstitious would count
This ominous, when it merely comes by chance.

SCENE THREE　　　　　　MODERN

It's a cold night – and yet you're sweating.

ANTONIO: I have been consulting the stars, to help find the Duchess's jewels.

BOSOLA: Ah, and how did they respond to your questions? Did they uncover the root of the mystery?
ANTONIO: What business is it of yours? It would be better to question what your purpose is in wandering around at night when everyone's been ordered to stay in their rooms.

BOSOLA: In truth, I'll tell you: I thought the devil wouldn't be out here while there's no one around, and so I came out here to say my prayers in peace. If that offends you, then you're a proper courtier.

ANTONIO: [Aside] This chap will be the ruin of me. [End aside.] You gave the Duchess apricots today. You better hope they weren't poisoned.

BOSOLA: Poisoned! How dare you accuse me of such a thing!

ANTONIO: Traitors are always confident until their treachery is exposed. There were jewels stolen too. In my mind, you're a more likely suspect than anyone else.

BOSOLA: You're a dishonest steward.
ANTONIO: Naughty slave, I'll take you down.

BOSOLA: When you do, I will fall on you and crush you to pieces.
ANTONIO: You are a rude snake indeed, sir. Are you cold-blooded, and do you have venom ready to squirt?
BOSOLA: ...
ANTONIO: You're great at telling lies.
BOSOLA: No, sir. Write out anything I've told you and I will swear an oath of its truthfulness.

ANTONIO: [Aside} I've got a nosebleed. Superstitious people would think this a sinister omen, but it's only a coincidence.

Two letters, that are wrought here for my name,
Are drown'd in blood!
Mere accident.—For you, sir, I'll take order
I' the morn you shall be safe.—[Aside.] 'Tis that must colour
Her lying-in.—Sir, this door you pass not:
I do not hold it fit that you come near
The duchess' lodgings, till you have quit yourself.—
[Aside.] The great are like the base, nay, they are the same,
When they seek shameful ways to avoid shame. [*Exit.*]

  BOS: Antonio hereabout did drop a paper:—
Some of your help, false friend. —O, here it is.
What's here? A child's nativity calculated! [*Reads.*]
'The duchess was deliver'd of a son, 'tween the hours
twelve and one in the night, Anno Dom. 1504,'—that's
this year—'decimo nono Decembris,'—that's this night—
'taken according to the meridian of Malfi,'—that's our
duchess: happy discovery!—'The lord of the first house
being combust in the ascendant, signifies short life; and
Mars being in a human sign, joined to the tail of the
Dragon, in the eighth house, doth threaten a violent
death. Cætera non scrutantur.'

Why, now 'tis most apparent; this precise fellow
Is the duchess' bawd:—I have it to my wish!
This is a parcel of intelligency
Our courtiers were cas'd up for: it needs must follow
That I must be committed on pretence
Of poisoning her; which I'll endure, and laugh at.
If one could find the father now! But that
Time will discover. Old Castruccio
I' th' morning posts to Rome: by him I'll send
A letter that shall make her brothers' galls
O'erflow their livers. This was a thrifty way!

SCENE THREE                    MODERN

Ah, but on my handkerchief – the initials of my name embroidered on it are now covered in nose blood! It's just a coincidence, not an omen. [*Aside ends.*] For you, sir – I'll have you arrested in the morning. [*Aside*] That will distract from the Duchess staying in her room. [*Aside ends.*] I do not think it appropriate for you to come near the Duchess's rooms until you've been proven innocent of any misdemeanour. [*Aside*] People of high status are the same as those of low status – they all do shameful things in order to avoid having their shameful natures exposed. [*Exit.*]


BOSOLA: Antonio dropped a bit of paper as he was leaving – lantern, help me find it with your light. Here it is. What is it? Oh, a child's horoscope! [*Reads*] '*the Duchess gave birth to a son, between the hours of twelve and one in the night, 1504 A.D.*' – that's this year – '*on the twelfth of December*' – that's tonight – '*recorded according to the longitudinal line passing through the province of Malfi*' – that's our Duchess! Gosh, what a thing to discover – she's had a baby! '*The planet influencing the boy's life is burned up, being too close to the sun, and this signifies the boy will have a short life. The planet Mars joins with one of the human constellations and with the tail of a dragon, in the eight astrological house, which suggests the boy's life will end with a violent death. Anything else is too obscure to be certain about.*'
Well, now it's obvious: this Antonio is the Duchess's pimp and he's been helping her get hooked up with someone. It's just as I wished! This is the precious piece of information responsible for everyone being locked up in their rooms tonight. Obviously Antonio's going to have me arrested for poisoning the Duchess, to cover up her childbirth, but that won't bother me. If only I could find out who the father is! But it will come out in time. Old Castruchio is riding to Rome in the morning: I'll send with him a letter whose contents will really upset Ferdinand and the Cardinal! This all happened nice and easily!

75  Though lust do mask in ne'er so strange disguise,
   She's oft found witty, but is never wise. [*Exit.*]

---

**WHAT'S GOING ON?**
*Bosola and Antonio bump into each other in the darkness outside the Duchess's palace during a scene that powerfully escalates the sense of threat and deception — both men are equally deceptive here. Bosola's crucial discovery of the news that the Duchess has given birth once again does not come*

---

Scene Four

[*Enter* CARDINAL *and* JULIA]

CARD: Sit: thou art my best of wishes. Prithee, tell me
What trick didst thou invent to come to Rome
Without thy husband?
JULIA:    Why, my lord, I told him
I came to visit an old anchorite
Here for devotion.
5   CARD:    Thou art a witty false one,—
I mean, to him.
JULIA: You have prevail'd with me
Beyond my strongest thoughts; I would not now
Find you inconstant.
CARD:    Do not put thyself
To such a voluntary torture, which proceeds
Out of your own guilt.
JULIA:    How, my lord!

SCENE FOUR                    MODERN

Although lust hides in all sorts of strange disguises, which make it enticing, it never manages to be wise. [*Exit.*]

---

*from his Machiavellian cunning, but due to a clumsy accident on the panicked Antonio's part when he drops the baby's horoscope. Plotwise, it's a catastrophe, and the audience anticipate things going sharply downhill for the Duchess and Antonio. Bosola, in frantic pursuit of his reward, immediately plans to contact Ferdinand with the news.*

---

[*Enter* CARDINAL *and* JULIA — *the Cardinal's lodgings in Rome.*]

CARDINAL: Sit down: you are the one thing I most wished for. Please, tell me, what excuse did you give your husband for coming to Rome without him?
JULIA: Why, my lord, I told him I was coming to visit a religious hermit, to spend time with him in devotion to God.
CARDINAL: You're a clever, deceptive one. Deceptive to your husband, I mean.

JULIA: You have been more of an influence over me than my own strongest thoughts — but I now I worry about your faithfulness toward me.
CARDINAL: Don't torture yourself just because you're feeling guilty.
JULIA: What do you mean?

CARD: You fear
My constancy, because you have approv'd
Those giddy and wild turnings in yourself.

JULIA: Did you e'er find them?

CARD: Sooth, generally for women,
A man might strive to make glass malleable,
Ere he should make them fixed.

JULIA: So, my lord.
CARD: We had need go borrow that fantastic glass
Invented by Galileo the Florentine
To view another spacious world i' th' moon,
And look to find a constant woman there.
JULIA: This is very well, my lord.
CARD: Why do you weep?
Are tears your justification? The self-same tears
Will fall into your husband's bosom, lady,
With a loud protestation that you love him
Above the world. Come, I'll love you wisely,
That's jealously; since I am very certain
You cannot make me cuckold.

JULIA: I'll go home
To my husband.
CARD: You may thank me, lady,
I have taken you off your melancholy perch,
Bore you upon my fist, and show'd you game,
And let you fly at it.—I pray thee, kiss me.—
When thou wast with thy husband, thou wast watch'd
Like a tame elephant:—still you are to thank me:—
Thou hadst only kisses from him and high feeding;
But what delight was that? 'Twas just like one
That hath a little fing'ring on the lute,
Yet cannot tune it:—still you are to thank me.
JULIA: You told me of a piteous wound i' th' heart,
And a sick liver, when you woo'd me first,
And spake like one in physic.
CARD: Who's that?—

SCENE FOUR                    MODERN

CARDINAL: The only reason you're worried about my faithfulness is because of your own unfaithfulness — toward your husband.
JULIA: But have I ever given you any cause to doubt my faithfulness toward you?
CARDINAL: It's a general truth for women: a man could just as easily make glass bendy as make women fixed [faithful].
JULIA: You really think so?
CARDINAL: We'd have to use a telescope, invented by Galileo the Florentine, and point it to another planet if we hope to find a faithful woman.

JULIA: Very good, my lord.
CARDINAL: Why are you crying? Are tears your way of trying to show your sincerity? But you'll cry the same tears in front of your husband, lady, with a loud protest that you love him above anyone else. Come, I'll love you wisely. It's wise for me to be jealous of your husband, because by not being your husband I can be certain you can't make me a cuckold [a man whose wife cheats on him].
JULIA: I'm going home to my husband.

CARDINAL: You should thank me. You're like a tamed bird, and I've freed you from the miserable perch of your dull marriage and shown you a good time. Please, kiss me. When you were with your husband, you were just watched like an elephant in a circus — again, you should thank me — you were given kisses only as if they were morsels of food fed to you. What joy was there in that? It was as if you were a lute played by a clumsy musician, out of tune. You should thank me.
JULIA: When we first met, you told me about how deeply you felt for me, and spoke as if you were lovesick.

CARDINAL: Who's there?

75

[*Enter* Servant]

40 Rest firm, for my affection to thee,
Lightning moves slow to 't.

---

### WHAT'S GOING ON?

*Webster uses the Cardinal and Julia's illicit relationship to contrast the Duchess and Antonio's. This one is full of distrust, with Julia and the Cardinal suspicious of each other's disloyalty. The Cardinal is coldly oppressive toward Julia, his speech peppered with old*

---

SERV. Madam, a gentleman,
That 's come post from Malfi, desires to see you.
CARD: Let him enter: I 'll withdraw. [Exit.]
SERV. He says
Your husband, old Castruccio, is come to Rome,
45 Most pitifully tir'd with riding post. [*Exit.*]

[*Enter* DELIO]

JULIA: [aside.] Signior Delio! 'tis one of my old suitors.
DELIO. I was bold to come and see you.
JULIA: Sir, you are welcome.

DELIO. Do you lie here?

JULIA: Sure, your own experience
Will satisfy you no: our Roman prelates
Do not keep lodging for ladies.

50 DELIO. Very well:
I have brought you no commendations from your husband,
For I know none by him.
JULIA: I hear he 's come to Rome.
DELIO. I never knew man and beast, of a horse and a knight,

76

SCENE FOUR                      MODERN

[*Enter* Servant.]
Be reassured: my affection for you makes lightning look slow in comparison.

---

*misogynistic tropes such as the woman being a wild creature needing to be tamed by the male. This scene also highlights the corruption of this figure of supposed spiritual authority.*

---

SERVANT: Madam, a gentleman arrived from Malfi wants to see you.
CARDINAL: Let him enter: I'll hide out of sight.
SERVANT: He says your husband, old Castruchio, has come to Rome and is exhausted after a fast ride.    [*Exit.*]

[*Enter* DELIO.]

JULIA: [*Aside*] Sir Delio! He was once romantically interested in me.

DELIO: Sorry for my boldness in coming to you.
JULIA: Sir, you are welcome.
DELIO: Are you staying here?
JULIA: You know that can't be the case, as high-ranking members of the Catholic church like the Cardinal do not keep rooms for ladies to stay in.
DELIO: Very well. I haven't brought any message from your husband, because I didn't hear of any he wanted to send.

JULIA: I hear he's come to Rome.
DELIO: I've never known a man and beast so sick of each other as Castruchio and his horse.

So weary of each other. If he had a good back,
55 He would have undertook to have borne his horse,
His breech was so pitifully sore.
  JULIA:      Your laughter
Is my pity.
  DELIO. Lady, I know not whether
You want money, but I have brought you some.

  JULIA: From my husband?
  DELIO.     No, from mine own allowance.
60 JULIA: I must hear the condition, ere I be bound to take it.
  DELIO. Look on 't, 'tis gold; hath it not a fine colour?
  JULIA: I have a bird more beautiful.
  DELIO.     Try the sound on 't.
  JULIA: A lute-string far exceeds it.
65 It hath no smell, like cassia or civet;
Nor is it physical, though some fond doctors
Persuade us seethe 't in cullises. I 'll tell you,
This is a creature bred by—

  [*Re-enter* Servant]

  SERV.     Your husband 's come,
Hath deliver'd a letter to the Duke of Calabria
That, to my thinking, hath put him out of his wits.
[*Exit.*]
70 JULIA: Sir, you hear:
Pray, let me know your business and your suit
As briefly as can be.
  DELIO. With good speed: I would wish you,
At such time as you are non-resident
With your husband, my mistress.
75 JULIA: Sir, I 'll go ask my husband if I shall,
And straight return your answer. [*Exit.*]
  DELIO.     Very fine!
Is this her wit, or honesty, that speaks thus?
I heard one say the duke was highly mov'd
With a letter sent from Malfi. I do fear

ACT TWO  ORIGINAL

If your husband didn't have a dodgy back, he'd have carried his horse rather than ride it, his bottom was so sore.

JULIA: Your mockery of him makes me ashamed to be married to him.
DELIO: Lady, I don't know if you need money, but I've brought you some.
JULIA: From my husband?
DELIO: No, it's my own money.
JULIA: I must hear your conditions before I accept it.

DELIO: Look at it — it's gold. Isn't it an attractive colour?
JULIA: I have a bird more beautiful than your gold.
DELIO: Listen to the coins clinking together.
JULIA: The sound of a lute being played is prettier. It doesn't have any nice smell, like spice or perfume, and it doesn't help with illness — although some greedy doctors persuade us to boil it in expensive medicinal soup. I'll tell you, money is a creature bred by —

[*Re-enter* Servant.]

SERVANT: Your husband's arrived; he has delivered a letter to Duke Ferdinand who, it seems to me, has been sent out of his mind by it. [*Exit.*]

JULIA: Sir, you hear my husband's come. Please, quickly tell me what you want from me.

DELIO: I want you to be my mistress when you're away from your husband.

JULIA: Sir, I'll go and ask my husband for permission, and will return with an answer. [*Exit.*]
DELIO: Very fine! Is she joking about asking her husband, or serious? I heard someone say Ferdinand was very upset by a letter sent from Malfi. I'm worried

ORIGINAL ACT TWO

80 Antonio is betray'd. How fearfully
Shows his ambition now! Unfortunate fortune!
They pass through whirl-pools, and deep woes do shun,
Who the event weigh ere the action's done. [*Exit.*]

## WHAT'S GOING ON?
*We might feel a bit sorry for Julia by now — every man she meets uses her in some way, even Delio, who's quite odd proposition for her to be his mistress is probably*

Scene Five

[*Enter* CARDINAL *and* FERDINAND *with a letter.*]

FERD: I have this night digg'd up a mandrake.

CARD: Say you?
FERD: And I am grown mad with 't.
CARD: What's the prodigy?

FERD: Read there,—a sister damn'd: she's loose i' the hilts;
Grown a notorious strumpet.
CARD: Speak lower.
FERD: Lower!
5 Rogues do not whisper 't now, but seek to publish 't
(As servants do the bounty of their lords)
Aloud; and with a covetous searching eye,
To mark who note them. O, confusion seize her!

SCENE FIVE                    MODERN

Antonio's secret has been discovered. This is the danger that comes from his ambition! Such bad luck! But it's people who avoid danger are the ones who weigh up the consequences of actions before proceeding with them. [*Exit.*]

*made so he can keep tabs on the Cardinal through her – he previously promised to Antonio he would find out anything that might keep Antonio safe.*

[*Enter* CARDINAL *and* FERDINAND *with the letter sent by Bosola with news of the Duchess giving birth.*]
FERDINAND: I feel as if I have dug up a mandrake [a plant said to provoke hallucinogenic effects if ingested, and in myth its roots, when dug up, are said to shriek and send mad anyone who hears it].
CARDINAL: What are you on about?
FERDINAND: And it's send me mad.
CARDINAL: What unnatural event has caused you to feel like this?
FERDINAND: Read this letter about a sister damned to hell. She's out of control. She's become a legendary whore.
CARDINAL: Speak more quietly!
FERDINAND: Quietly! Scoundrels aren't talking quietly about it now, but are making it publicly known as loudly as they can, just as servants boast about the generosity of their lords while looking around at which important people notice them. Oh, confusion make her suffer!

    She hath had most cunning bawds to serve her turn,
10 And more secure conveyances for lust
    Than towns of garrison for service.
      CARD:    Is 't possible?
    Can this be certain?
      FERD:    Rhubarb, O, for rhubarb
    To purge this choler! Here 's the cursèd day
    To prompt my memory; and here 't shall stick
15 Till of her bleeding heart I make a sponge
    To wipe it out.
      CARD:    Why do you make yourself
    So wild a tempest?

      FERD:    Would I could be one,
    That I might toss her palace 'bout her ears,
    Root up her goodly forests, blast her meads,
20 And lay her general territory as waste
    As she hath done her honours.
      CARD:    Shall our blood,
    The royal blood of Arragon and Castile,
    Be thus attainted?
      FERD:    Apply desperate physic:
    We must not now use balsamum, but fire,
25 The smarting cupping-glass, for that 's the mean
    To purge infected blood, such blood as hers.
    There is a kind of pity in mine eye,—
    I 'll give it to my handkercher; and now 'tis here,
    I 'll bequeath this to her bastard.

      CARD:    What to do?
30 FERD: Why, to make soft lint for his mother's wounds,
    When I have hew'd her to pieces.

      CARD:    Curs'd creature!
    Unequal nature, to place women's hearts
    So far upon the left side!

SCENE FIVE                    MODERN

She has crafty pimps to help satisfy her lust, and has more secret arrangements for lustful encounters than towns have for receiving supplies.
CARDINAL: Is this really true? For certain?

FERDINAND: I need some medicinal rhubarb to purge this sickness! This cursed day written in Bosola's letter (the day of the child's birth) will always be stained in my memory, and it will stay there until I use her bleeding heart as a sponge to wipe it away.
CARDINAL: Why are you getting yourself into such a tempest of emotion?
FERDINAND: I wish I could be a tempest so I could blast down her palace around her ears, uproot her forests, blast away her meadows, and make the same wasted ruin of her territory as she has made of her honour.

CARDINAL: Will our precious family bloodline, the royal blood of Arragon and Castille, be tainted by this?

FERDINAND: We must apply urgent medicine to her tainted blood. We must not now use gentle treatments, but ferociously effective ones, like the painfully hot glasses pressed against skin to draw out disease — that's the way to cleanse infected blood like hers. I'm crying — I'll give this tear to my handkerchief, and now it's there, I'll give it as an inheritance to her bastard child.
CARDINAL: Why would you do such a thing?
FERDINAND: So he can make a soft bandage for his mother's wounds after I have hacked her to pieces.
CARDINAL: Cursed creature! It is unfair of nature to put women's hearts too far on the left side of their bodies, where the hearts of fools lie. [He alludes to a passage from Ecclesiastes: "The heart of the wise inclines to the right, but the heart of the fool to the left".]

FERD: Foolish men,
That e'er will trust their honour in a bark
35 Made of so slight weak bulrush as is woman,
Apt every minute to sink it!
   CARD: Thus ignorance, when it hath purchas'd honour,
It cannot wield it.
   FERD: Methinks I see her laughing,—
Excellent hyena! Talk to me somewhat quickly,
40 Or my imagination will carry me
To see her in the shameful act of sin.
   CARD: With whom?
   FERD: Happily with some strong-thigh'd bargeman,
Or one o' th' wood-yard that can quoit the sledge
45 Or toss the bar, or else some lovely squire
That carries coals up to her privy lodgings.
   CARD: You fly beyond your reason.
   FERD: Go to, mistress!
'Tis not your whore's milk that shall quench my wild-fire,
But your whore's blood.
50    CARD: How idly shows this rage, which carries you,
As men convey'd by witches through the air,
On violent whirlwinds! This intemperate noise
Fitly resembles deaf men's shrill discourse,
Who talk aloud, thinking all other men
To have their imperfection.
55    FERD: Have not you
My palsy?
   CARD: Yes, [but] I can be angry
Without this rupture. There is not in nature
A thing that makes man so deform'd, so beastly,
As doth intemperate anger. Chide yourself.
60 You have divers men who never yet express'd
Their strong desire of rest but by unrest,
By vexing of themselves. Come, put yourself
In tune.

## SCENE FIVE — MODERN

FERDINAND: It's men who are the fools, for trusting their honour to a ship made of such flimsy material as women are made of, always at risk of sinking it!

CARDINAL: Stupid people like her can't keep hold of honour when they obtain it.

FERDINAND: I'm imagining her laughing, just like a hyena. Talk to me about something, quickly, or I'll start imagining her having sex.

CARDINAL: With whom?

FERDINAND: Probably with some strong-thighed boatman, or one of the woodcutters who can swing the sledgehammer or throw the timber around. Or some knight's attendant who carries coal up to her private chambers.

CARDINAL: You're becoming irrational.

FERDINAND: Go to hell, mistress! It's not your whore's milk that will calm my raging emotions, but your whore's blood.

CARDINAL: This rage of yours is useless. It's carrying you into turmoil, just like men under the spell of witches. Your foul-tempered ramblings are like the nonsensical speech of deaf men, who think all other men talk in the same imperfect way as them.

FERDINAND: Do you not have my illness? Don't you also feel my rage?

CARDINAL: Yes, but I can be angry without your hysteria and lack of self-control. There is nothing in nature that makes man so deformed and beastly as hysterical anger. Discipline yourself. Rise above the many men who can only demonstrate their strong need for self-control by demonstrating their complete lack of it. Pull yourself together.

FERD: So I will only study to seem
The thing I am not. I could kill her now,
65 In you, or in myself; for I do think
It is some sin in us heaven doth revenge
By her.

CARD: Are you stark mad?
FERD:       I would have their bodies
Burnt in a coal-pit with the ventage stopp'd,
That their curs'd smoke might not ascend to heaven;
70 Or dip the sheets they lie in in pitch or sulphur,
Wrap them in 't, and then light them like a match;
Or else to-boil their bastard to a cullis,
And give 't his lecherous father to renew
The sin of his back.
CARD:       I 'll leave you.
FERD:       Nay, I have done.
75 I am confident, had I been damn'd in hell,
And should have heard of this, it would have put me
Into a cold sweat. In, in; I 'll go sleep.
Till I know who leaps my sister, I 'll not stir:
That known, I 'll find scorpions to string my whips,
80 And fix her in a general eclipse.    [*Exeunt.*]

---

## WHAT'S GOING ON?

*The brothers' different reactions to the news of the Duchess giving birth sharply highlight their different characters. The Cardinal is briefly and unemotionally concerned about his family bloodline being tainted, before his concern shifts to Ferdinand who's in a wildly*

SCENE FIVE　　　　　　　MODERN

FERDINAND: Then I will study how to outwardly seem composed, when deep down I am far from it. I could kill her now by killing you, or by killing myself, as we all share the same blood, and I think God is using her to get revenge for the sinful nature of our blood.

CARDINAL: Are you completely out of your mind?

FERDINAND: I want their (the Duchess's and her lover's) bodies burned in a coal pit with the chimney blocked up so that their cursed souls can't climb to heaven. Or I'll dip their bedsheets in pitch or sulphur, wrap them up, and then set fire to them. Or I'll boil their bastard baby until it becomes a soup, and feed it to the lustful father to revenge his lustful sin.

CARDINAL: I'm getting out of here.

FERDINAND: There's no need; I'm finished. I am confident this news would have put me in a cold sweat even if I were sat damned in the burning heat of hell. Go, go; I'll go to sleep. I'll do nothing else until I know who is having sex with my sister. When I know, I'll find scorpions and put their sting on my whip, and use it plunge her into total darkness.

*[Exeunt.]*

---

*emotional mess ranging from jealousy — seen most starkly when he imagines his sister having sex — to violent fury. In being driven so heavily by emotion, Ferdinand fills the stereotype that would have been more commonly held against women during Webster's time.*

---

## Act Three

Scene One

[*Enter* ANTONIO *and* DELIO]

ANT: Our noble friend, my most beloved Delio!
O, you have been a stranger long at court:
Came you along with the Lord Ferdinand?
　DEL: I did, sir: and how fares your noble duchess?
5　ANT: Right fortunately well: she's an excellent
Feeder of pedigrees; since you last saw her,
She hath had two children more, a son and daughter.
DEL: Methinks 'twas yesterday. Let me but wink,
And not behold your face, which to mine eye
10 Is somewhat leaner, verily I should dream
It were within this half hour.
　ANT: You have not been in law, friend Delio,
Nor in prison, nor a suitor at the court,
Nor begg'd the reversion of some great man's place,
15 Nor troubled with an old wife, which doth make
Your time so insensibly hasten.
　DEL:　　Pray, sir, tell me,
Hath not this news arriv'd yet to the ear
Of the lord cardinal?
　ANT:　　I fear it hath:
The Lord Ferdinand, that's newly come to court,
Doth bear himself right dangerously.
20　DEL:　　Pray, why?
　ANT: He is so quiet that he seems to sleep
The tempest out, as dormice do in winter.
Those houses that are haunted are most still
Till the devil be up.
　　DEL:　　What say the common people?

SCENE ONE         MODERN

[*Enter* ANTONIO *and* DELIO — *a couple of years have passed since the end of Act Two.*]

ANTONIO: My noble friend, my most beloved Delio! Oh, you've been away from court for a long time. Did you come here with Ferdinand?
DELIO: I did, sir. How is your noble duchess?
ANTONIO: Very well, fortunately. She's an excellent breeder of pedigrees; since you last saw her, she's given birth to two more children, a son and a daughter.

DELIO: It seems to me as if it were only yesterday when I last saw her. It's as if I've just winked and your face has suddenly looked thinner and older. I swear it was only in this last half hour I last saw you.
ANTONIO: You've not been in the law courts, friend Delio, nor in prison, nor trying to get noticed at court, nor been begging for the inheritance of some great man's estate, nor have you been bothered by an old wife, and that's why time seems to have gone so quickly for you.

DELIO: Please, sir, tell me: has the news of the Duchess's children not yet reached the ears of the Cardinal?

ANTONIO: I'm worried it may have done. I noticed Ferdinand, when he arrived here at court, behaving very...dangerously.
DELIO: In what way?

ANTONIO: He is very quiet, as if he is waiting for a storm to pass, or hibernating like mice to see the winter through. He is like a haunted house, quiet and still, waiting for evil to fill and wake it.
DELIO: What's the gossip among the commoners?

25 ANT: The common rabble do directly say
She is a strumpet.
DEL:   And your graver heads
Which would be politic, what censure they?
ANT: They do observe I grow to infinite purchase,
The left hand way; and all suppose the duchess
30 Would amend it, if she could; for, say they,
Great princes, though they grudge their officers
Should have such large and unconfined means
To get wealth under them, will not complain,
Lest thereby they should make them odious
35 Unto the people. For other obligation
Of love or marriage between her and me
They never dream of.
DEL:   The Lord Ferdinand
Is going to bed.

[*Enter* DUCHESS, FERDINAND, BOSOLA *and* Attendants]
FERD:   I'll instantly to bed,
For I am weary.—I am to bespeak
A husband for you.
40 DUCH:   For me, sir! Pray, who is 't?
FERD: The great Count Malatesti.
DUCH:   Fie upon him!
A count! He's a mere stick of sugar-candy;
You may look quite through him. When I choose
A husband, I will marry for your honour.
FERD: You shall do well in 't.—How is 't, worthy
45 Antonio?

DUCH: But, sir I am to have private conference with you
About a scandalous report is spread
Touching mine honour.
FERD:   Let me be ever deaf to 't:
One of Pasquil's paper-bullets, court-calumny.
50 A pestilent air, which princes' palaces

SCENE ONE                    MODERN

ANTONIO: The common people call the Duchess a prostitute.

DELIO: And the wiser people, who should be more sensible – what opinion do they give?

ANTONIO: They say I have acquired wealth in an underhanded way, and they all suppose the Duchess would correct it if she could, but she can't because, as they say, great rulers like her might not like it when their servants get rich under them, but they can't complain or do anything about it because it would make them unpopular with the other ordinary people. No one has any suspicion of any relationship or marriage between her and me.

DELIO: Ferdinand's off to bed.

[*Enter* DUCHESS, FERDINAND, BOSOLA *and* Servants.]

FERDINAND: I'm going straight to bed, because I'm exhausted after the journey. I'm going to arrange a husband for you.

DUCHESS: For me, sir?! Please tell me, who is it?

FERDINAND: The great Count Malatesti.

DUCHESS: Oh no, not him! A count? He's nothing more than a stick of candy, so slim and flimsy in substance that you could see right through him. I'll choose my own husband, and I'll choose one that won't damage the family honour.

FERDINAND: You'll do well in doing this. [Ambiguous – could mean "you'll choose well" or "you'll be well/better of if you do indeed choose for my honour".] How's things, Antonio?

DUCHESS: But sir, I need to speak with you privately about a scandalous rumour that's threatening my reputation.

FERDINAND: Don't pay any attention to it. It'll just be some satirical attack [Pasquil was a satirist], just normal courtly slander.

Are seldom purg'd of. Yet, say that it were true,
I pour it in your bosom, my fix'd love
Would strongly excuse, extenuate, nay, deny
Faults, were they apparent in you. Go, be safe
In your own innocency.
55 DUCH:   [Aside] O bless'd comfort!
This deadly air is purg'd.  Exeunt [DUCHESS,
ANTONIO, DELIO, and Attendants.]

---

### WHAT'S GOING ON?
*The structure of the play starts to get pretty crazy – Webster slips in jokes about this with Delio saying it only feels like a brief moment since he saw Antonio (true for the audience in the theatre) when in the play's timeline it's been a couple of years.*

*The levels of deception also mount up, with the Duchess pretending not to be married, and Ferdinand*

---

FERD:   Her guilt treads on
Hot burning cultures. Now, Bosola,
How thrives our intelligence?

BOS:   Sir, uncertainly:
'Tis rumour'd she hath had three bastards, but
By whom we may go read i' the stars.
60 FERD:   Why, some
Hold opinion all things are written there.
BOS: Yes, if we could find spectacles to read them.
I do suspect there hath been some sorcery
Us'd on the duchess.
FERD:   Sorcery! to what purpose?
65 BOS: To make her dote on some desertless fellow
She shames to acknowledge.
FERD:   Can your faith give way
To think there 's power in potions or in charms,

SCENE ONE        MODERN

It might seem unpleasant, but it's normal in all rulers' courts. But, even if it were true, I tell you sincerely that my unshakeable love for you would absolutely excuse – no, would refuse to believe – you were guilty of any faults. Go, be confident in your own innocence.

DUCHESS: [*Aside*] Oh, thank goodness. My worries are gone.
[*Exeunt* DUCHESS, ANTONIO, DELIO.]

---

*pretending he doesn't know she's a mother. Interestingly, she rejects Ferdinand's proposed husband merely on the grounds of his material qualities, which wasn't a factor that affected her choice of Antonio. It seems a bit naïve of her to be so quickly reassured by Ferdinand's dismissal of the gossip about her.*

---

FERDINAND: She's as guilty as a wife forced to walk barefoot over burning plough blades. [Ferdinand refers to a medieval test of fidelity – if the wife's feet got burned, she was deemed to have cheated on her husband. If unburned, she was innocent.] Now, Bosola, what information have you found out?
BOSOLA: Sir, nothing certain. It's rumoured she has given birth to three illegitimate children, but we might as well consult the stars to learn who fathered them.
FERDINAND: Well, some people think all knowledge is contained in the stars.
BOSOLA: Yes, if we knew how to decipher them. I suspect some magic has been used on the Duchess.
FERDINAND: Magic?! For what purpose?
BOSOLA: To make her fall in love with some undeserving fellow who she's too ashamed to make public.
FERDINAND: Do you really believe it's possible that potions and spells

To make us love whether we will or no?
  BOS: Most certainly.
70 FERD: Away! these are mere gulleries, horrid things,
Invented by some cheating mountebanks
To abuse us. Do you think that herbs or charms
Can force the will? Some trials have been made
In this foolish practice, but the ingredients
75 Were lenitive poisons, such as are of force
To make the patient mad; and straight the witch
Swears by equivocation they are in love.
The witch-craft lies in her rank blood. This night
I will force confession from her. You told me
80 You had got, within these two days, a false key
Into her bed-chamber.
  BOS:     I have.
  FERD:     As I would wish.
  BOS: What do you intend to do?
  FERD:     Can you guess?
  BOS:    No.
  FERD: Do not ask, then:
He that can compass me, and know my drifts,
85 May say he hath put a girdle 'bout the world,
And sounded all her quick-sands.
  BOS:     I do not
Think so.
  FERD:     What do you think, then, pray?
  BOS:     That you
Are your own chronicle too much, and grossly
Flatter yourself.
  FERD:     Give me thy hand; I thank thee:
90 I never gave pension but to flatterers,
Till I entertained thee. Farewell.
That friend a great man's ruin strongly checks
Who rails into his belief all his defects. [*Exeunt.*]

SCENE ONE              MODERN

can make us love someone against our own will?
BOSOLA: Most certainly.
FERDINAND: Nonsense! The things you talk of are just tricks for gullible people, horrid things invented by cheating scoundrels to exploit us. Do you think herbs and charms can override our own will? Some tests have been done about this foolish practice. The ingredients were soothing in taste but poisonous, and made the patient mad, allowing the witch to swear the patient was in love when he only appeared to be. It's the Duchess's potent blood that has this bewitching power, not magic. Tonight I will force a confession from her. You told me you had obtained, within the last two days, a duplicate key to her bedroom.

BOSOLA: I have.
FERDINAND: I want it.
BOSOLA: What do you intend to do?
FERDINAND: Can you guess?

BOSOLA: No.
FERDINAND: Then don't ask. If someone can claim to understand me, and understand my intentions, then he can claim to understand all the mysteries in the world.

BOSOLA: I don't think so.

FERDINAND: Then please tell me what do you think?
BOSOLA: That you big yourself up too much.

FERDINAND: Shake my hand. I thank you. I only gave attention to flatterers until I started listening to you. Farewell. A true friend can prevent a great man being ruined by forcing him to recognise his failings.   [*Exeunt.*]

> **WHAT'S GOING ON?**
> *For Ferdinand, female desire is akin to witchcraft — evil, destructive to men, unnatural. Despite his bold claims that he has more wisdom than anyone could ever*

Scene Two

   [*Enter* DUCHESS, ANTONIO, *and* CARIOLA.]

  DUCH: Bring me the casket hither, and the glass.—
You get no lodging here to-night, my lord.
  ANT: Indeed, I must persuade one.
    DUCH:     Very good:
I hope in time 'twill grow into a custom,
5  That noblemen shall come with cap and knee
To purchase a night's lodging of their wives.
  ANT: I must lie here.
    DUCH:     Must! You are a lord of mis-rule.

  ANT: Indeed, my rule is only in the night.
    DUCH: To what use will you put me?
  ANT:     We 'll sleep together.
10  DUCH: Alas, what pleasure can two lovers find in sleep?
  CARI: My lord, I lie with her often, and I know
She 'll much disquiet you.
  ANT:     See, you are complain'd of.
  CARI: For she 's the sprawling'st bedfellow.

SCENE TWO        MODERN

*understand, he doesn't seem to have any clear, rational plan beyond making his sister confess — likely because he is driven by jealous emotion rather than rational logic.*

[*Enter* DUCHESS, ANTONIO, *and* CARIOLA — *in the Duchess's chamber.*]

DUCHESS: Bring me the makeup, and the mirror — you won't be sleeping here tonight, Antonio.
ANTONIO: Then I'll have to persuade you.
DUCHESS: That's good — I hope it will become normal that noblemen must beg to sleep with their wives.

ANTONIO: I must sleep here.
DUCHESS: Must?! You are a lord of misrule [the title of the servant who led revelries on the twelfth night of Christmas, when it was custom in wealthy household for the servants and nobles to make a game out of swapping roles for one night].
ANTONIO: Indeed, it's only at night I can rule over you.
DUCHESS: How will you use me?
ANTONIO: We'll just sleep next to each other.
DUCHESS: But what pleasure can two lovers get from just sleeping?
CARIOLA: Antonio, I sleep with her often, and I know she'll disturb you.
ANTONIO: See how people complain about you.
CARIOLA: She'll disturb you because she sprawls all over you in her sleep.

ANT: I shall like her the better for that.
15  CARI: Sir, shall I ask you a question?
ANT: I pray thee, Cariola.
CARI: Wherefore still when you lie with my lady
Do you rise so early?

ANT:     Labouring men
Count the clock oft'nest, Cariola,
Are glad when their task 's ended.
20  DUCH: I 'll stop your mouth. [*Kisses him.*]

ANT: Nay, that 's but one; Venus had two soft doves
To draw her chariot; I must have another.— [*he kisses her.*]
When wilt thou marry, Cariola?
CARI:     Never, my lord.
ANT: O, fie upon this single life! forgo it.
25 We read how Daphne, for her peevish [flight,]
Became a fruitless bay-tree; Syrinx turn'd
To the pale empty reed; Anaxarete
Was frozen into marble: whereas those
Which married, or prov'd kind unto their friends,
30 Were by a gracious influence transhap'd
Into the olive, pomegranate, mulberry,
Became flowers, precious stones, or eminent stars.
CARI: This is a vain poetry: but I pray you, tell me,
If there were propos'd me, wisdom, riches, and beauty,
35 In three several young men, which should I choose?
ANT: 'Tis a hard question. This was Paris' case,
And he was blind in 't, and there was a great cause;
For how was 't possible he could judge right,
Having three amorous goddesses in view,
40 And they stark naked? 'Twas a motion
Were able to benight the apprehension
Of the severest counsellor of Europe.
Now I look on both your faces so well form'd,
It puts me in mind of a question I would ask.
CARI: What is 't?
45  ANT:     I do wonder why hard-favour'd ladies,

SCENE TWO  MODERN

ANTONIO: I'll like her more if she does that.
CARIOLA: Antonio, can I ask you a question?
ANTONIO: Please do.
CARIOLA: Why, when you sleep with the Duchess, do you still rise so early? [i.e. get up so early, but clearly intended as innuendo.]
ANTONIO: Working men keep their eye on the clock, Cariola, and leave as soon as their work is finished.

DUCHESS: I'll stop your stupid jokes (by stopping your mouth with a kiss).
ANTONIO: One kiss isn't enough — the goddess of love had two soft doves to drive her carriage; I must have a second. [*Kisses her.*] When are you going to get married, Cariola?
CARIOLA: Never.
ANTONIO: Oh, the single life is no good. Abandon it. Think of the stories of Daphne, transformed into a fruitless tree as punishment for running away from someone who desired her. For the same reason, Syrinx was transformed into a reed in a river and Anaxarete was turned into stone. On the other hand, other women who embraced marriage where transformed into beautiful things full of life, or precious jewels or important stars.

CARIOLA: These are meaningless stories. But, please tell me, if I had the choice of a wise man, a rich man, or a beautiful man to marry, which should I choose?

ANTONIO: That's a hard one. It was the same choice Paris had to make when he had to name the fairest between Aphrodite, Hera and Athena. He had no idea how to choose, and understandably so — how could he think straight when confronted by three amorous and naked goddesses? It was a sight able to cloud the judgement of the most serious thinker in Europe. Now I look at both your well-formed faces, I'm reminded of a question I want to ask.

CARIOLA: What is it?
ANTONIO: I wonder why it is that unattractive ladies,

ORIGINAL ACT THREE

For the most part, keep worse-favour'd waiting-women
To attend them, and cannot endure fair ones.
   DUCH: O, that 's soon answer'd.
Did you ever in your life know an ill painter
50 Desire to have his dwelling next door to the shop
Of an excellent picture-maker? 'Twould disgrace
His face-making, and undo him. I prithee,
When were we so merry?—My hair tangles.

---

### WHAT'S GOING ON?
*This is all about showing the blissful harmony of the Duchess and Antonio's marriage. Webster aligns the audience with the concept of sexually liberated woman (challenging for the Jacobean audience) via the playful innuendos, which come across as light-hearted and affectionate rather than crude.*

---

   ANT: Pray thee, Cariola, let 's steal forth the room,
55 And let her talk to herself: I have divers times
Serv'd her the like, when she hath chaf'd extremely.
I love to see her angry. Softly, Cariola. [*Exeunt* ANTONIO
*and* CARIOLA.]
   DUCH: Doth not the colour of my hair 'gin to change?
When I wax gray, I shall have all the court
60 Powder their hair with arras, to be like me.
You have cause to love me; I ent'red you into my heart
   [*Enter* FERDINAND *unseen*]
Before you would vouchsafe to call for the keys.
We shall one day have my brothers take you napping.
Methinks his presence, being now in court,
65 Should make you keep your own bed; but you 'll say
Love mix'd with fear is sweetest. I 'll assure you,
You shall get no more children till my brothers
Consent to be your gossips. Have you lost your tongue?
'Tis welcome:
70 For know, whether I am doom'd to live or die,
I can do both like a prince.

SCENE TWO              MODERN

in the main, keep even more unattractive maids and don't like attractive ones.

DUCHESS: Oh, that's easy to answer. Did you ever know of a bad painter who wanted to live next to a good one? It would highlight how bad his own artwork is, and ruin him. I ask you, when have we been so happy as this? My hair's tangled.

---

*But is the Duchess guilty of vanity here? Not only is she looking at herself in the mirror, but she's also preoccupied with her private life — rather than her public role. These things lead her to being caught off guard in the next moments...*

---

ANTONIO: [*Whispering to* Cariola] Hey, Cariola, let's sneak out of the room without her noticing, and let her talk to herself. I've played this sort of practical joke loads of times and it's really annoyed her. I do love to see her angry. [*They hide.*]

DUCHESS: Isn't the colour of my hair beginning to change? When it turns grey, I will have all the court powder their hair with white, so they look as aged as me. You have an obligation to love me, because I allowed you into my heart [*enter* FERDINAND *without her seeing*] before you had asked for permission to be there. One day my brothers will find you napping in my chamber. I think Ferdinand's presence in court is good reason for you to sleep in your own room, but I know you'll just say the danger adds excitement. I assure you you'll get no more children until my brothers agree to be their godparents ["gossips"]. Why aren't you saying anything? [*Notices* FERDINAND *in the mirror.*] I'm glad you're here.

Know that whether you intend for me do live or die, I can do both with the integrity of a prince.

FERD: Die, then, quickly! Giving her a poniard.
Virtue, where art thou hid? What hideous thing
Is it that doth eclipse thee?
　DUCH: Pray, sir, hear me.
　FERD: Or is it true thou art but a bare name,
And no essential thing?
　DUCH: Sir—
75　FERD: Do not speak.
　DUCH: No, sir:
I will plant my soul in mine ears, to hear you.
　FERD: O most imperfect light of human reason,
That mak'st [us] so unhappy to foresee
80 What we can least prevent! Pursue thy wishes,
And glory in them: there's in shame no comfort
But to be past all bounds and sense of shame.

　DUCH: I pray, sir, hear me: I am married.

　FERD: So!
　DUCH: Happily, not to your liking: but for that,
85 Alas, your shears do come untimely now
To clip the bird's wings that's already flown!
Will you see my husband?
　FERD: Yes, if I could change
Eyes with a basilisk.
　DUCH: Sure, you came hither
By his confederacy.
　FERD: The howling of a wolf
90 Is music to thee, screech-owl: prithee, peace.—
Whate'er thou art that hast enjoy'd my sister,
For I am sure thou hear'st me, for thine own sake
Let me not know thee. I came hither prepar'd
To work thy discovery; yet am now persuaded
95 It would beget such violent effects
As would damn us both. I would not for ten millions
I had beheld thee: therefore use all mean
I never may have knowledge of thy name;
Enjoy thy lust still, and a wretched life,

SCENE TWO    MODERN

FERDINAND: Die, then, quickly. Virtue, where are you hiding? What hideous thing is this that keeps you hidden?

DUCHESS: Please, listen to me.
FERDINAND: Or is it true that you, virtue, are nothing more than a name and don't actually exist?

DUCHESS: Sir —
FERDINAND: Do not speak.
DUCHESS: No, I will listen, and give your words all my attention.
FERDINAND: Oh, how flawed is human reasoning, that it makes us predict the things we least want to happen and that we can't do anything to change, as I predicted you would take a husband. Pursue what you want, and find glory in it, because the only comfort of being in shame is you're no longer able to feel shame.
DUCHESS: Please, listen. I've not done anything shameful — I'm legitimately married.
FERDINAND: Oh really!
DUCHESS: Perhaps not to someone who you'd approve of, but it's too late for you to stop it. Will you meet my husband?

FERDINAND: Yes, if I could swap my eyes with a basilisk, so that I could kill him by just looking at him.

DUCHESS: Surely he arranged for you to come here.

FERDINAND: The howling of a wolf is music compared to your screeching voice. Please, be quiet — [*calls out loudly*] whoever you are who's had sex with my sister, for I'm sure you're within hearing distance, for your own sake make sure I never find you out. I came here prepared to discover who you are, but now I worry it would result in such violence that we would both be damned to hell. Not even for the sake of ten million [referring to money, or perhaps number of people's lives] would I want to lay eyes on you, and therefore do whatever you need to ensure I never learn your name. Enjoy your lust with my sister, but on the condition of having a miserable life.

<sup>100</sup> On that condition.—And for thee, vile woman,
If thou do wish thy lecher may grow old
In thy embracements, I would have thee build
Such a room for him as our anchorites
To holier use inhabit. Let not the sun
<sup>105</sup> Shine on him till he 's dead; let dogs and monkeys
Only converse with him, and such dumb things
To whom nature denies use to sound his name;
Do not keep a paraquito, lest she learn it;
If thou do love him, cut out thine own tongue,
Lest it bewray him.

<sup>110</sup>  DUCH:    Why might not I marry?
I have not gone about in this to create
Any new world or custom.
  FERD:    Thou art undone;
And thou hast ta'en that massy sheet of lead
That hid thy husband's bones, and folded it
About my heart.

  DUCH:    Mine bleeds for 't.
<sup>115</sup>  FERD:    Thine! thy heart!
What should I name 't unless a hollow bullet
Fill'd with unquenchable wild-fire?
  DUCH:    You are in this
Too strict; and were you not my princely brother,
I would say, too wilful: my reputation
Is safe.

<sup>120</sup>  FERD:  Dost thou know what reputation is?
I 'll tell thee,—to small purpose, since the instruction
Comes now too late.
Upon a time Reputation, Love, and Death,
Would travel o'er the world; and it was concluded
<sup>125</sup> That they should part, and take three several ways.
Death told them, they should find him in great battles,
Or cities plagu'd with plagues: Love gives them counsel
To inquire for him 'mongst unambitious shepherds,
Where dowries were not talk'd of, and sometimes
<sup>130</sup> 'Mongst quiet kindred that had nothing left

SCENE TWO        MODERN

And for you, vile woman, if you want your playboy to grow old in your arms, I suggest you build a room as secluded as the ones monks inhabit. Don't let him see sunlight until he's dead. Let dogs and monkeys be the only things to talk to him, and such dumb animals be the only ones to say his name. Don't keep a parrot, in case she learns to repeat his name. If you do indeed love him, cut out your own tongue to prevent you accidentally revealing his name to me.


DUCHESS: Why shouldn't I marry? There's nothing unconventional about a widow getting remarried.

FERDINAND: You are ruined. And you have taken that lead sheet that cover's your dead first husband's bones and wrapped it around my heart [implying, perhaps accidentally, that Ferdinand loves her as much as her first husband did].
DUCHESS: My heart bleeds for yours.
FERDINAND: Your heart?! What should I call it apart from a hollow bullet filled with burning acid and fired at me?

DUCHESS: Your feelings are too intense, and if you weren't my brother, I'd say you were jealous. My reputation is safe.


FERDINAND: Do you even know what reputation is? I'll tell you — not that there's much point, seeing as yours is already lost. Once upon a time Reputation, Love and Death travelled all over the world until they decided they should go their separate ways. Death said they would find him in great battles, or cities plagued with disease.


Love said he would be among humble shepherds, who talk of marriage but never money, and sometimes among quiet siblings who have been left no inheritance by their dead parents.

ORIGINAL   ACT THREE

By their dead parents: "Stay,' quoth Reputation,
'Do not forsake me; for it is my nature,
If once I part from any man I meet,
I am never found again.' And so for you:
135 You have shook hands with Reputation,
And made him invisible. So, fare you well:
I will never see you more.
    DUCH:    Why should only I,
Of all the other princes of the world,
Be cas'd up, like a holy relic? I have youth
And a little beauty.
140 FERD:    So you have some virgins
That are witches. I will never see thee more. [*Exit.*]

---

### WHAT'S GOING ON?
*Turns out Ferdinand didn't have much of a plan — he comes to rant and rage, all emotional — but he's terrifying too, partly because he's so unstable and also because he makes such violent threats against the Duchess and her husband.*

---

[*Re-enter* ANTONIO *with a pistol, and* CARIOLA]
    DUCH: You saw this apparition?
    ANT:    Yes: we are
Betray'd. How came he hither? I should turn
This to thee, for that.
    CARI:    Pray, sir, do; and when
145 That you have cleft my heart, you shall read there
Mine innocence.
    DUCH:    That gallery gave him entrance.
  ANT: I would this terrible thing would come again,
That, standing on my guard, I might relate
My warrantable love.— [*She shows the poniard.*]
      Ha! what means this?
    DUCH: He left this with me.
150 ANT:    And it seems did wish
You would use it on yourself.
    DUCH:    His action seem'd

SCENE TWO　　　　　　　MODERN

Reputation said "stay, don't leave me alone, for it is in my nature that once I leave anyone I meet I am never found again." And this is the case for you: you have shook hands and said goodbye to reputation, therefore losing it forever. So, good bye. I will not ever see you again.


DUCHESS: Why should I be the only ruler in the whole world to be locked up like a holy relic in a museum? I'm still young and beautiful — why shouldn't I marry?

FERDINAND: Your youth and beauty are devils. I will not ever see you again. [*Exit.*]

*His irrationality looks particularly stark when the Duchess asks the very sensible question — what's the big deal about me getting married? He can only answer with more senseless ranting, because there is no rational answer. The real reason he's so upset — that he desires her himself — is detected by the Duchess when she suggests he might be jealous.*

　　　　　[Re-enter ANTONIO, *with a pistol, and* CARIOLA.]
DUCHESS: Did you see that apparition of Ferdinand?

ANTONIO: Yes. Our secret's out. How did he know to come here? I suspect you're to blame, Cariola.

CARIOLA: Please sir, blame me, and when you've punished me by cutting out my heart, you'll find the mark of my innocence on it.

DUCHESS: He must have come by the gallery corridor, which isn't locked.
ANTONIO: I would like him to come again, so that I could prove my love. [*She shows him the dagger.*] Ah! What does this mean?
DUCHESS: He left it for me.

ANTONIO: And it seems he wanted you to kill yourself with it.
DUCHESS: His behaviour suggested as much.

107

To intend so much.
  ANT:     This hath a handle to 't,
As well as a point: turn it towards him, and
So fasten the keen edge in his rank gall. [*Knocking within.*]
How now! who knocks? More earthquakes?
155  DUCH:     I stand
As if a mine beneath my feet were ready
To be blown up.
  CARI:     'Tis Bosola.
  DUCH:     Away!
O misery! methinks unjust actions
Should wear these masks and curtains, and not we.
160 You must instantly part hence: I have fashion'd it already.
[*Exit* ANTONIO.]

    [*Enter* BOSOLA.]


  BOS: The duke your brother is ta'en up in a whirlwind;
Hath took horse, and 's rid post to Rome.
  DUCH:     So late?
  BOS: He told me, as he mounted into the saddle,
You were undone.
  DUCH:     Indeed, I am very near it.
165  BOS: What 's the matter?
  DUCH: Antonio, the master of our household,
Hath dealt so falsely with me in 's accounts.
My brother stood engag'd with me for money
Ta'en up of certain Neapolitan Jews,
170 And Antonio lets the bonds be forfeit.
  BOS: Strange!–[*Aside*] This is cunning.
  DUCH:     And hereupon
My brother's bills at Naples are protested
Against.–Call up our officers.
  BOS:     I shall. [*Exit.*]
    [*Re-enter* ANTONIO]

  DUCH: The place that you must fly to is Ancona:
175 Hire a house there; I 'll send after you

SCENE TWO         MODERN

ANTONIO: This knife has a handle you can use to wield it; turn the blade toward him, and fasten it in his bitter insides. [*Knocking at the door.*] What now?! More catastrophes?

DUCHESS: I feel as if I'm standing on a landmine ready to blow up.

CARIOLA: It's Bosola at the door.

DUCHESS: Send him away! Oh misery! I feel people who have done unjust things should be the ones who have to hide away, not us. Antonio, you have to get far away from here. I've already planned a cover story.

[*Exit* ANTONIO.]

[*Enter* BOSOLA.]

BOSOLA: Your brother seems extremely upset. He's taken his horse and dashed off to Rome.
DUCHESS: At this hour?
BOSOLA: He told me, as he climbed into the saddle, you were ruined.
DUCHESS: Indeed, I am very near it.
BOSOLA: What's the matter?
DUCHESS: Antonio, the steward, has messed up my finances. Ferdinand sorted out a loan of money for me from some Neapolitan Jews, and Antonio failed to pay the money back.

BOSOLA: [*Aside*] This is a clever deceit.

DUCHESS: And therefore the lenders are demanding the payment from Ferdinand. Call the officers.

BOSOLA: I shall. [*Exit.*]
[*Re-enter* ANTONIO.]

DUCHESS: You must flee to Ancona and rent a house there. I'll send my valuables after you. Our fragile safety depends

My treasure and my jewels. Our weak safety
Runs upon enginous wheels: short syllables
Must stand for periods. I must now accuse you
Of such a feigned crime as Tasso calls
180 *Magnanima menzogna*, a noble lie,
'Cause it must shield our honours.—Hark! they are coming.
[Re-enter BOSOLA and Officers]

  ANT: Will your grace hear me?
    DUCH: I have got well by you; you have yielded me
A million of loss: I am like to inherit
185 The people's curses for your stewardship.
You had the trick in audit-time to be sick,
Till I had sign'd your quietus; and that cur'd you
Without help of a doctor.—Gentlemen,
I would have this man be an example to you all;
190 So shall you hold my favour; I pray, let him;
For h'as done that, alas, you would not think of,
And, because I intend to be rid of him,
I mean not to publish.—Use your fortune elsewhere.
  ANT: I am strongly arm'd to brook my overthrow,
195 As commonly men bear with a hard year.
I will not blame the cause on 't; but do think
The necessity of my malevolent star
Procures this, not her humour. O, the inconstant
And rotten ground of service! You may see,
200 'Tis even like him, that in a winter night,
Takes a long slumber o'er a dying fire,
A-loth to part from 't; yet parts thence as cold
As when he first sat down.
    DUCH:     We do confiscate,
Towards the satisfying of your accounts,
All that you have.
205  ANT:     I am all yours; and 'tis very fit
All mine should be so.
    DUCH:    So, sir, you have your pass.
  ANT: You may see, gentlemen, what 'tis to serve
A prince with body and soul. [*Exit.*]

upon us being clever. We don't have time to speak for long. I must now accuse you of a pretend crime of the sort the sixteenth-century Italian poet Tasso called a "noble lie" to help protect the vulnerable from abuse, and to protect our reputation. Listen! They're coming.

*[Re-enter BOSOLA and Officers]*

ANTONIO: Will you listen to me?
DUCHESS: You have served me well – you've given me such a magnificent loss that I will inherit the people's curses for your dodgy stewardship. When we were auditing my finances you pretended to be sick until I gave approval of your arrangements, and that magically cured you without a doctor. You have manipulated me. Gentlemen, I want this Antonio to be an example for all of you, so you will keep my approval of you. I ask you to leave him alone. He has done things you wouldn't dream to do, and because I intend to get rid of him, I ask you not to tell anyone about it. Publish your gossip about other things.

ANTONIO: I am well prepared to tolerate my downfall, as it's common for men like me to cope with hard times. I will not look to blame anyone for the cause of my demise: I think the wicked stars are what have brought it about rather than the Duchess's character. Oh, the inconstancy and rotten nature of being a servant! A servant is like him who sleeps next to a dying fire on a winter night, not wanting to leave it, and yet having to leave as cold, with as little reward, as when he first sat down. (A servant is never rewarded.)

DUCHESS: I'm confiscating the rest of your money to help straighten up the accounts.
ANTONIO: I belong to you, and so it's right that my belongings are also yours.

DUCHESS: So, sir, you are free to go.
ANTONIO: You can see, gentleman, what it's like to serve a ruler with all your body and soul. *[Exit.]*

BOS: Here's an example for extortion: what moisture is
210 drawn out of the sea, when foul weather comes, pours
down, and runs into the sea again.
 DUCH: I would know what are your opinions
Of this Antonio.
 SEC. OFF. He could not abide to see a pig's head gaping:
215 I thought your grace would find him a Jew.

 THIRD OFF. I would you had been his officer, for your
own sake.

 FOURTH OFF. You would have had more money.
 FIRST OFF. He stopped his ears with black wool, and to
220 those came to him for money said he was thick of hearing.
 SEC. OFF. Some said he was an hermaphrodite, for he
could not abide a woman.
 FOURTH OFF. How scurvy proud he would look when
the treasury was full! Well, let him go.

225 FIRST OFF. Yes, and the chippings of the buttery fly
after him, to scour his gold chain.


 DUCH: Leave us. [*Exeunt* Officers.]
What do you think of these?
 BOS: That these are rogues that in 's prosperity,
But to have waited on his fortune, could have wish'd
230 His dirty stirrup riveted through their noses,
And follow'd after 's mule, like a bear in a ring;
Would have prostituted their daughters to his lust;
Made their first-born intelligencers; thought none happy
But such as were born under his blest planet,
235 And wore his livery: and do these lice drop off now?

Well, never look to have the like again:
He hath left a sort of flattering rogues behind him;
Their doom must follow. Princes pay flatterers
In their own money: flatterers dissemble their vices,

SCENE TWO                    MODERN

BOSOLA: Here's a good lesson: what goes around comes around.

DUCHESS: I'd like to hear your opinions of Antonio.

SECOND OFFICER: I always thought he was a Jew. [Distasteful, but reflects the antisemitism of the period. Orthodox Jews do not eat pork.]
THIRD OFFICER: I wish you had been supervising him, for your own sake.

FOURTH OFFICER: You would have had more money.
FIRST OFFICER: He blocked up his ears with black wool, and told anyone who asked him for money that he couldn't hear them.
SECOND OFFICER: There's rumour that Antonio had both male and female reproductive organs, because he was never with a woman.
FOURTH OFFICER: How disgustingly proud he looked when the treasury was full of money! It's no loss to see him go.
FIRST OFFICER: Yes, and let the powder used to polish gold go with him, so he can polish his gold chain [the badge worn by a treasurer].
DUCHESS: Leave us alone. [*Exeunt* Officers.] Bosola, what do you think of these officers?
BOSOLA: That they are rogues who, when Antonio was prosperous, would have done anything for him, would even have wanted his dirty stirrup to be riveted through their noses, and followed after his mule like a bear in a circus ring; they would have made their daughters Antonio's prostitutes, and made their babies spy for him; they would think no one could be happy unless born under the same blessed astrological sign as Antonio, and would have worn his uniform. Now that Antonio's not prosperous, these parasites drop off him. He should never look to have their sort around him again; he leaves behind him a lot of sycophantic scoundrels and their own downfall must follow. Princes get from sycophants what sycophants get from princes: sycophants deny their princes have weaknesses,

240 And they dissemble their lies; that 's justice.
Alas, poor gentleman!

    DUCH: Poor! he hath amply fill'd his coffers.

  BOS: Sure, he was too honest. Pluto, the god of riches,
When he 's sent by Jupiter to any man,
245 He goes limping, to signify that wealth
That comes on God's name comes slowly; but when he 's sent
On the devil's errand, he rides post and comes in by scuttles.
Let me show you what a most unvalu'd jewel
You have in a wanton humour thrown away,
250 To bless the man shall find him. He was an excellent
Courtier and most faithful; a soldier that thought it
As beastly to know his own value too little
As devilish to acknowledge it too much.
Both his virtue and form deserv'd a far better fortune:
His discourse rather delighted to judge itself than show
255 itself:
His breast was fill'd with all perfection,
And yet it seemed a private whisp'ring-room,
It made so little noise of 't.
    DUCH: But he was basely descended.
  BOS: Will you make yourself a mercenary herald,
260 Rather to examine men's pedigrees than virtues?
You shall want him:
For know an honest statesman to a prince
Is like a cedar planted by a spring;
The spring bathes the tree's root, the grateful tree
265 Rewards it with his shadow: you have not done so.
I would sooner swim to the Bermoothes on
Two politicians' rotten bladders, tied
Together with an intelligencer's heart-string,
Than depend on so changeable a prince's favour.
270 Fare thee well, Antonio! Since the malice of the world
Would needs down with thee, it cannot be said yet

SCENE TWO         MODERN

and the princes deny their sycophants are lying to them: that's fair. Alas, poor Antonio!
DUCHESS: Poor?! He has made plenty of money over the time in my service.
BOSOLA: I think he was too honest. Wealth that comes in the right way comes slowly. Wealth that's wrongfully obtained comes quickly. Let me show you what an unappreciated jewel was Antonio, whom you have thrown away in hysterical passion, and whom will bless whoever next finds him.

He was an excellent and faithful courtier. He was a soldier who knew it was as bad to be too modest as it is to be too arrogant. Both his goodness and his character deserved a better fate. When he spoke he found more delight in criticising himself than being boastful. His heart was pure, and yet it never made a big deal about being so pure.

DUCHESS: But he is of low social status.
BOSOLA: Will you make yourself a defender of rank and status, preferring to value men for their pedigree rather than their goodness? You will miss him, for know that an honest advisor for a prince is like a spring of water for a newly planted cedar tree. The spring feeds the tree's roots, and the grateful tree rewards the spring with shade. You have not rewarded him. I would rather float to Bermuda on two politician's rotten inflated bladders, tied

together with a spy's heart-string, than depend on someone with such unreliable favour as you.
Fare well, Antonio! Since the wickedness of the world has decided to ruin you, it cannot be said that any damage has

That any ill happen'd unto thee, considering thy fall
Was accompanied with virtue.
    DUCH: O, you render me excellent music!
    BOS:    Say you?
275   DUCH: This good one that you speak of is my husband.
    BOS: Do I not dream? Can this ambitious age
Have so much goodness in 't as to prefer
A man merely for worth, without these shadows
Of wealth and painted honours? Possible?
    DUCH: I have had three children by him.
280   BOS:    Fortunate lady!
For you have made your private nuptial bed
The humble and fair seminary of peace,
No question but: many an unbenefic'd scholar
Shall pray for you for this deed, and rejoice
285 That some preferment in the world can yet
Arise from merit. The virgins of your land
That have no dowries shall hope your example
Will raise them to rich husbands. Should you want
Soldiers, 'twould make the very Turks and Moors
290 Turn Christians, and serve you for this act.
Last, the neglected poets of your time,
In honour of this trophy of a man,
Rais'd by that curious engine, your white hand,
Shall thank you, in your grave, for 't; and make that
295 More reverend than all the cabinets
Of living princes. For Antonio,
His fame shall likewise flow from many a pen,
When heralds shall want coats to sell to men.
    DUCH: As I taste comfort in this friendly speech,
So would I find concealment.
300   BOS: O, the secret of my prince,
Which I will wear on th' inside of my heart!

SCENE TWO         MODERN

been done to you, seeing as you're still virtuous and haven't become wicked like the world that's destroyed you.
DUCHESS: Oh, this is music to my ears!
BOSOLA: What do you mean?

DUCHESS: This good man you speak about is my husband.

BOSOLA: Am I dreaming? Can this ambitious world yet have enough goodness in it to prefer a man for his worth, and disregard these meaningless superficial things of wealth and honour? Is it really possible?
DUCHESS: He and I have had three children together.

BOSOLA: You wonderful lady! You have made your wedding bed a place for the humble nurturing of peace, no doubt about it. Many unappreciated and unrewarded people will praise you for what you've done, and celebrate that some reward can still come to people who truly merit it. The unmarried women of your land who have no wealth to offer a husband will hope your example will bring rich husbands to them. If you ever want more soldiers, soldiers from distant lands and different religions will become Christians and fight for you thanks to what you've done.

Lastly, the unappreciated poets of your time will be inspired to lift their pens by your marriage to this trophy of a man, and will write about you even when you're dead, and their writing will make your grave seem more respected than all the palaces of living princes. For Antonio, his reputation will also be respected by many poets' pens, when people who have false/paid-for honour will have to buy respect.

DUCHESS: Although I'm comforted by your friendly words, I hope you can keep the secret safe.

BOSOLA: I will keep it safe in my heart!

DUCH: You shall take charge of all my coin and jewels,
And follow him; for he retires himself
To Ancona.
   BOS:      So.
     DUCH:         Whither, within few days,
I mean to follow thee.
305 BOS:        Let me think:
I would wish your grace to feign a pilgrimage
To our Lady of Loretto, scarce seven leagues
From fair Ancona; so may you depart
Your country with more honour, and your flight
310 Will seem a princely progress, retaining
Your usual train about you.
     DUCH:        Sir, your direction
Shall lead me by the hand.
   CARI:      In my opinion,
She were better progress to the baths at Lucca,
Or go visit the Spa
315 In Germany; for, if you will believe me,
I do not like this jesting with religion,
This feigned pilgrimage.
       DUCH: Thou art a superstitious fool:
Prepare us instantly for our departure.
Past sorrows, let us moderately lament them,
320 For those to come, seek wisely to prevent them. [*Exeunt*
DUCHESS *and* CARIOLA.]
   BOS: A politician is the devil's quilted anvil;
He fashions all sins on him, and the blows
Are never heard: he may work in a lady's chamber,
As here for proof. What rests but I reveal
325 All to my lord? O, this base quality
Of intelligencer! Why, every quality i' the world
Prefers but gain or commendation:
Now, for this act I am certain to be rais'd,
And men that paint weeds to the life are prais'd.  [Exit.]

SCENE TWO            MODERN

DUCHESS: You will look after all my valuables, and take them to Antonio in Ancona.

BOSOLA: I will.
DUCHESS: I will follow you there in a few days' time.

BOSOLA: Let me think: I suggest you pretend to go on a pilgrimage to the shrine of our Lady of Loretto, which isn't far from fair Ancona. This will serve as a cover story allowing you to leave your country honourably, and your journey will seem an honourable one, with your usual attendants around you.

DUCHESS: I trust your instruction.

CARIOLA: In my opinion, it would be better to go to the baths at Lucca, or the Spa in Germany, because, believe me, it is wrong to treat religion in such a joking way as to fake a pilgrimage.

DUCHESS: You're a superstitious idiot, Cariola. Prepare us for an immediate departure. Let us feel moderately sad about bad things that have happened in the past and look carefully for ways to prevent more bad things happening in the future.
                [*Exeunt* DUCHESS *and* CARIOLA.]
BOSOLA: A cunning person softens the blows of the devil's hammer — the cunning person can do terrible things and make it so no one hears about them, even in a lady's private chamber, as I've just proven. What else is there for me to do apart from reveal everything to Ferdinand? Oh, this lowly role of spy! But even lowly deeds lead to some sort of gain or reward. For this act I am certain to be rewarded, just as artists that paint pictures of lowly subjects like weeds are rewarded. [*Exit.*]

ORIGINAL                        ACT THREE

### WHAT'S GOING ON?
*It's a clear indication of the morally inverted world Webster shapes that the Duchess finds success in being dishonest (her deceitful cover story about Antonio's corruption sends him away to safety) and finds doom in being honest (her confession to Bosola that Antonio is her husband will spark her downfall).*

*And how did Bosola worm it out of her? By being honest about Antonio. (Being honest really doesn't lead to good things in this world!) Bosola seems to identify*

Scene Three

[*Enter* CARDINAL, FERDINAND, MALATESTI, PESCARA, DELIO, *and* SILVIO.]

CARD: Must we turn soldier, then?
MAL.    The emperor,
Hearing your worth that way, ere you attain'd
This reverend garment, joins you in commission
With the right fortunate soldier the Marq is of Pescara,
And the famous Lannoy.
5   CARD:      He that had the honour
Of taking the French king prisoner?
MAL.    The same.
Here's a plot drawn for a new fortification
At Naples.
[CARDINAL *and* MALATESTE *turn aside to study the plans.*]

FERD: This great Count Malatesti, I perceive,

SCENE THREE          MODERN

*with Antonio as someone who hasn't been fairly rewarded, and praises him with apparent sincerity.*

*The dishonest officers are just the sort of people that have been criticised throughout the play, even since Antonio's first speech about the French court – they are the "flatterers" who only tell the Duchess what they think she wants to hear rather than the truth. Webster identifies this as being a core part of an unhealthy, corrupt political system.*

[*Enter* CARDINAL, FERDINAND, MALATESTI, PESCARA, DELIO, *and* SILVIO – *an army camp in Rome.*]

CARDINAL: Must I become a solder, then?
MALATESTE: The emperor has heard what a worthy solider you were before you became a cardinal, and has assigned you a military commission alongside Marquis Pescara and the famous Lannoy.

CARDINAL: Lannoy was the one who captured the French king?
MALATESTE: That's him. Look - here are some architectural plans for a new fortress at Naples.
 [CARDINAL *and* MALATESTI *turn aside to study the plans.*]

FERDINAND: This great Count Malateste – am I to

Hath got employment?
　　DELIO.　　No employment, my lord;
10　A marginal note in the muster-book, that he is
　A voluntary lord.
　　FERD:　　He 's no soldier.
　　DELIO. He has worn gun-powder in 's hollow tooth for
　the toothache.
　　SIL. He comes to the leaguer with a full intent
15　To eat fresh beef and garlic, means to stay
　Till the scent be gone, and straight return to court.
　　DELIO. He hath read all the late service
　As the City-Chronicle relates it;
　And keeps two pewterers going, only to express
　Battles in model.
20　SIL.　　Then he 'll fight by the book.

　DELIO. By the almanac, I think,
To choose good days and shun the critical;
That 's his mistress' scarf.
　　SIL.　　Yes, he protests
He would do much for that taffeta.
25　DELIO. I think he would run away from a battle,
To save it from taking prisoner.
　　SIL.　　He is horribly afraid
Gun-powder will spoil the perfume on 't.
　　DELIO. I saw a Dutchman break his pate once
For calling him pot-gun; he made his head
30　Have a bore in 't like a musket.




　SIL. I would he had made a touch-hole to 't.
He is indeed a guarded sumpter-cloth,
Only for the remove of the court.

SCENE THREE                    MODERN

understand he has been employed by the king?
DELIO: No, my lord. There's only small mention of him in the army registry book, noting that he has volunteered to help the war efforts.
FERDINAND: He's no soldier.

DELIO: His only experience with gunpowder is putting it in his tooth to stop it aching.
SILVIO: He's come to the army camp fully intending to eat lots of fresh beef and garlic, will stay until the food's all gone, and then he'll go straight back to court.

DELIO: He reads about the battles in the news, and uses his toy soldiers, made by the pewterers he employs, to recreate the battles in model form.

SILVIO: Then he'll fight as if his only experience in war comes from reading about it in a book.
DELIO: In the book of astrology, I expect, so he'll know which are the safe days to join the fight and which are the dangerous ones to avoid. There's his mistress's scarf.
SILVIO: Yes, he claims he would do anything for that scarf [taffeta being the fine material it is made with].
DELIO: He's so cowardly I suspect he would flee from a battle to save his scarf being taken prisoner.
SILVIO: He is horribly afraid gunpowder will spoil the perfume on it.

DELIO: I once saw Malateste get punched in the head by a Dutchman who he'd called a braggart [a "pop-gun" was a type of gun that made lots of noise and was used mainly for firing salutes at ceremonies rather than in battle, and hence became idiomatic for someone who makes a lot of noise but lacks substance]. The dutchman put a whole in his head like a bullet-wound.
SILVIO: I wish it had been a cannonball rather than a bullet. Malateste is indeed nothing more than a pretty-looking cloth for horses' saddles — decorated and flimsy, and only good for moving with the court people from one place to another rather than joining in with battles.

ORIGINAL                                  ACT THREE

> **WHAT'S GOING ON?**
> *Malatesti is a minor character who Webster uses here for two important purposes: firstly, to show the vehemence of gossip in the courtly environment, and secondly, as another example of a "flatterer", similar to the officers in the previous scene.*

[*Enter* BOSOLA]
PES. Bosola arriv'd! What should be the business?
35 Some falling-out amongst the cardinals.
These factions amongst great men, they are like
Foxes, when their heads are divided,
They carry fire in their tails, and all the country
About them goes to wrack for 't.

SIL.    What 's that Bosola?
40 DELIO. I knew him in Padua,—a fantastical scholar, like such who study to know how many knots was in Hercules' club, of what colour Achilles' beard was, or whether Hector were not troubled with the tooth-ache. He hath studied himself half blear-eyed to know the true symmetry of
45 Cæsar's nose by a shoeing-horn; and this he did to gain the name of a speculative man.

PES. Mark Prince Ferdinand:
A very salamander lives in 's eye,
To mock the eager violence of fire.

50 SIL. That cardinal hath made more bad faces with his oppression than ever Michael Angelo made good ones. He lifts up 's nose, like a foul porpoise before a storm.

PES. The Lord Ferdinand laughs.
DELIO.    Like a deadly cannon
That lightens ere it smokes.
55 PES. These are your true pangs of death,
The pangs of life, that struggle with great statesmen.

SCENE THREE          MODERN

*Delio's and Silvio's comments make it clear that Malatesti is only trying to raise his own status, without contributing anything to the war effort.*

*The war they discuss never becomes an important aspect of the play's plot, but it is a fitting reflection of the more personal conflicts between the characters.*

[*Enter* BOSOLA.]
PESCARA: Bosola's here! What news does he bring? Probably about some argument among the cardinals. All these separate groups of people in power — they're like the foxes from the Bible story who had their tails tied together by Samson and burning torches fixed to them so they would destroy the fields of the Philistines they ran over. They run over the country and everything around them goes to ruin.
SILVIO: Who is this Bosola chap?
DELIO: I knew him in Padua — he was a scholar, but a fanciful, bizarre one, like the sort who study trivial details such as the number of knots in Hercules' club, or the colour of Achilles' beard, or whether Hector had toothache. He studied furiously to learn whether Julius Caesar's nose was perfectly symmetrical, and he did this just to get a reputation for being an intellectual, full of profound thought and insight.
PESCARA: Look at Ferdinand! He looks so furious it's as if a salamander, the lizard that's said to live in fire, is in his eye; the way he looks makes the violence of fire seem feeble in contrast to his own fury.
SILVIO: That Cardinal has made more people miserable with his tyranny than Michael Angelo painted good faces. Just as porpoises come up to the surface of the water before a coming storm, he raises up his nose and misery follows.
PESCARA: Now Ferdinand's laughing.
DELIO: He's laughing in the same way a cannon shows a cheerful spark when its fuse is lit and before it explodes.
PESCARA: We're seeing here the pains great statesmen feel as they struggle with the troubles of life.

ORIGINAL                    ACT THREE

   DELIO.  In such a deformed silence witches whisper their charms.
   CARD:  Doth she make religion her riding-hood
To keep her from the sun and tempest?


60  FERD:  That, that damns her. Methinks her fault and beauty,
Blended together, show like leprosy,
The whiter, the fouler. I make it a question
Whether her beggarly brats were ever christ'ned.


65  CARD:  I will instantly solicit the state of Ancona
To have them banish'd.
   FERD:      You are for Loretto:
I shall not be at your ceremony; fare you well.—
Write to the Duke of Malfi, my young nephew
She had by her first husband, and acquaint him
With 's mother's honesty.
   BOS:     I will.
70  FERD:     Antonio!
A slave that only smell'd of ink and counters,
And never in 's life look'd like a gentleman,
But in the audit-time.—Go, go presently,
Draw me out an hundred and fifty of our horse,
75  And meet me at the foot-bridge.        [*Exeunt.*]

---

### WHAT'S GOING ON?
*Bosola delivers his discovery — that Antonio is the Duchess's husband — to Ferdinand and the Cardinal. Webster's staging is really interesting here, because he focuses on Silvio and Delio, and we hear their voices when Bosola delivers his news, rather than Ferdinand's and the Cardinal's. It's another way of highlighting the role of gossip in this fickle courtly environment.*

---

SCENE THREE       MODERN

DELIO: The deformed noise of their quiet whispering is the same noise of witches whispering their spells.
CARDINAL: [Reacting to what he's been told by Bosola about the Duchess and Antonio, and the plan to fake a pilgrimage] does she treat religion as if it's a convenient piece of clothing she can wear when she needs protection?
FERDINAND: She'll go to hell as punishment. I think her flaws and her beauty, mixed together, take the appearance of leprosy, which turns the skin whiter the worse it gets. [i.e. the Duchess is making a show of doing something white/pure by going on pilgrimage, but beneath she is becoming more impure.] I do wonder if her beggarly bratty children are legitimately baptised if she treats religion so lightly as this.
CARDINAL: I will immediately arrange for them to be banished from Ancona.
FERDINAND: You're going to Loretto to catch her there, but I will not join you. [*To* BOSOLA] Write to the son she had with her first husband and tell him what her mother's done.


BOSOLA: I will.
FERDINAND: Antonio! A slave that only smelled of ink and counters [used in accounting work] and never looked like a proper gentleman except when counting other people's money. Fetch me a hundred and fifty of our horses, and meet me at the foot-bridge.
　　　[*Exeunt.*]

---

*The Cardinal's accusation of the Duchess using religion in an exploitative way comes across as quite hypocritical, considering the way he uses religion himself. While Ferdinand gets all steamed up about Antonio, the Cardinal begins his assault on the Duchess's sovereignty, planning to have her banished from the state of Ancona, which he has the power to do as Ancona was a papal state. The banishment ceremony forms the next scene.*

---

ORIGINAL                                        ACT THREE

Scene Four

[*Enter* Two Pilgrims *to the Shrine of our Lady of Loretto.*]

FIRST PIL.  I have not seen a goodlier shrine than this;
Yet I have visited many.
SEC. PIL.      The Cardinal of Arragon
Is this day to resign his cardinal's hat:
His sister duchess likewise is arriv'd
To pay her vow of pilgrimage. I expect
A noble ceremony.
FIRST PIL.      No question.—They come.

[Here the ceremony of the CARDINAL'S instalment, in the habit of a soldier, perform'd in delivering up his cross, hat, robes, and ring, at the shrine, and investing him with sword, helmet, shield, and spurs; then ANTONIO, the DUCHESS and their children, having presented themselves at the shrine, are, by a form of banishment in dumb-show expressed towards them by the CARDINAL and the state of Ancona, banished: during all which ceremony, this ditty is sung, to very solemn music, by divers churchmen: and then exeunt [all except the Two Pilgrims.]

*Arms and honours deck thy story,*
*To thy fame's eternal glory!*
*Adverse fortune ever fly thee;*
*No disastrous fate come nigh thee!*
*I alone will sing thy praises,*
*Whom to honour virtue raises,*
*And thy study, that divine is,*
*Bent to martial discipline is,*

SCENE FOUR                    MODERN


[Enter two pilgrims at the shrine of Our Lady of Loretto.]

FIRST PILGRIM: I've never seen a nicer shrine than this one, even though I've visited many.
SECOND PILGRIM: The Cardinal will today take off his cardinal's hat and replace it with a soldier's. His sister the Duchess is also here, as she has come on a pilgrimage. I expect it will be a noble ceremony.

FIRST PILGRIM: No doubt. Here they come.

[The ceremony of the Cardinal's instalment as a soldier involves attendants taking from him his cardinal's cross, hat, robes, ring, and placing them beside the shrine. They then dress him with a sword, helmet, shield, and spurs. Then ANTONIO, the DUCHESS, and their children, having presented themselves at the shrine, are shown to be banished from the state of Ancona by the CARDINAL in the form of a dumb-show [no actor speaks; all is shown through mime]. During this, the following song is sung by many religious people/pilgrims, and then all exeunt expect the two pilgrims.]


Weapons and glory decorate your story
In honour of your reputation's eternal glory
Bad luck stay away from you,
No disastrous fate come near you!
I alone will sing praises of you,
Your devoted studies of God
You now bend to study warfare.

15 *Lay aside all those robes lie by thee;*
*Crown thy arts with arms, they 'll beautify thee.*
*O worthy of worthiest name, adorn'd in this manner,*
*Lead bravely thy forces on under war's warlike banner!*
*O, mayst thou prove fortunate in all martial courses!*
20 *Guide thou still by skill in arts and forces!*
*Victory attend thee nigh, whilst fame sings loud thy powers;*
*Triumphant conquest crown thy head, and blessings pour down showers!*

    FIRST PIL. Here 's a strange turn of state! who would have thought
So great a lady would have match'd herself
25 Unto so mean a person? Yet the cardinal
Bears himself much too cruel.
    SEC. PIL.    They are banish'd.
    FIRST PIL. But I would ask what power hath this state
Of Ancona to determine of a free prince?
    SEC. PIL. They are a free state, sir, and her brother show'd
30 How that the Pope, fore-hearing of her looseness,
Hath seiz'd into th' protection of the church
The dukedom which she held as dowager.

    FIRST PIL. But by what justice?
    SEC. PIL.    Sure, I think by none,
Only her brother's instigation.
35     FIRST PIL. What was it with such violence he took
Off from her finger?
    SEC. PIL.    'Twas her wedding-ring;
Which he vow'd shortly he would sacrifice
To his revenge.
    FIRST PIL.    Alas, Antonio!
If that a man be thrust into a well,
40 No matter who sets hand to 't, his own weight
Will bring him sooner to th' bottom. Come, let 's hence.
Fortune makes this conclusion general,
All things do help th' unhappy man to fall.    [*Exeunt.*]

## SCENE FOUR — MODERN

*Lay aside all those religious robes,*
*Decorate yourself with weapons; they will make you beautiful.*
*You are of the most worthy status when decorated in this way,*
*Lead bravely your armies under war's warlike banner!*
*Oh, may you be lucky in all your military encounters!*
*Be guided by skill in cleverness and in brute force!*
*Victory will come to you soon, while stories spread of your power;*
*Triumphant victory will be your crown and blessings will rain down on you.*

FIRST PILGRIM: Here's a strange turn of events! Who would have thought so great a lady as the Duchess would have married such a lowly person as Antonio? Yet the Cardinal was too cruel to them.

SECOND PILGRIM: They are banished from Ancona.
FIRST PILGRIM: But what power does this state have over the sovereign ruler (the Duchess) of another state (Malfi)?
SECOND PILGRIM: Ancona is a state partly under the influence of the Pope [this is what "free state" means, ironically], and the Cardinal acted on the approval of the Pope, who, having heard of the Duchess's loose morals, took the dukedom of Malfi (which she received from her husband at his death) under the protection of the church.
FIRST PILGRIM: But how's that fair?
SECOND PILGRIM: I don't think it is. But the Cardinal deems it so.
FIRST PILGRIM: What was it he took so violently from her finger?
SECOND PILGRIM: It was her wedding ring; he swore he would dispose of it out of revenge.

FIRST PILGRIM: Poor Antonio! If he were thrown down a well, no matter who tried to pull him out, his own misfortune and mistakes would keep weighing him down. Come on, let's go. All things conspire to bring a man down: fate makes that true of all people.

                                                            [*Exeunt.*]

Scene Five

[*Enter* DUCHESS, ANTONIO, Children, CARIOLA, *and* Servants.]

DUCH: Banish'd Ancona!
ANT:     Yes, you see what power
Lightens in great men's breath.

DUCH:     Is all our train
Shrunk to this poor remainder?
ANT:     These poor men,
Which have got little in your service, vow
5  To take your fortune: but your wiser buntings,
Now they are fledg'd, are gone.

DUCH:     They have done wisely.
This puts me in mind of death: physicians thus,
With their hands full of money, use to give o'er
Their patients.
ANT:     Right the fashion of the world:
10  From decay'd fortunes every flatterer shrinks;
Men cease to build where the foundation sinks.

DUCH: I had a very strange dream to-night.
ANT:     What was 't?
DUCH: Methought I wore my coronet of state,
And on a sudden all the diamonds
Were chang'd to pearls.
15  ANT:     My interpretation
Is, you 'll weep shortly; for to me the pearls
Do signify your tears.
DUCH:     The birds that live i' th' field
On the wild benefit of nature live

SCENE FIVE        MODERN

[*Enter* DUCHESS, ANTONIO, *Children,* CARIOLA, *and* Servants — near the shrine.]

DUCHESS: How dreadful! We've been banished from Ancona!
ANTONIO: Yes, you see how the commands of great men have a power like lightning [or possibly a fire igniting/lighting].
DUCHESS: [Looking at the few people around her] is this all that's left of my servants?
ANTONIO: These poor men, who haven't been rewarded well for serving you, have promised to share whatever fate comes to you, whereas your wiser servants [compared to birds in "buntings"] have left the nest. They have left you; they are gone.
DUCHESS: They were wise to have done so. This makes me think of death. Those servants are like doctors who, once they've been paid by their patients, give up on the patients and leave them to die.
ANTONIO: That is exactly how the world works. People's loyalty to their masters comes in the form of superficial flattery, which soon ends when the master's fortune (wealth or luck) ends.
DUCHESS: I had a very strange dream last night.
ANTONIO: What was it?
DUCHESS: I dreamt I was wearing my crown, and all of a sudden the diamonds turned to pearls [a less precious variety of jewel].
ANTONIO: My interpretation is you'll cry soon, because the pearls represent tears.

DUCHESS: The birds in the fields, who rely on wild nature for survival,

133

Happier than we; for they may choose their mates,
20 And carol their sweet pleasures to the spring.

[*Enter* BOSOLA *with a letter*]

  BOS: You are happily o'erta'en.
    DUCH:     From my brother?
  BOS: Yes, from the Lord Ferdinand your brother
All love and safety.
    DUCH:     Thou dost blanch mischief,
Would'st make it white. See, see, like to calm weather
25 At sea before a tempest, false hearts speak fair
To those they intend most mischief. [*Reads.*]
'Send Antonio to me; I want his head in a business.'
A politic equivocation!
He doth not want your counsel, but your head;
30 That is, he cannot sleep till you be dead.
And here 's another pitfall that 's strew'd o'er
With roses; mark it, 'tis a cunning one: [*Reads.*]
'I stand engaged for your husband for several debts at
Naples: let not that trouble him; I had rather have his
35 heart than his money':—
And I believe so too.
    BOS:     What do you believe?
    DUCH: That he so much distrusts my husband's love,
He will by no means believe his heart is with him
Until he see it: the devil is not cunning enough
40 To circumvent us in riddles.
  BOS: Will you reject that noble and free league
Of amity and love which I present you?
    DUCH: Their league is like that of some politic kings,
Only to make themselves of strength and power
45 To be our after-ruin; tell them so.
  BOS: And what from you?
  ANT:     Thus tell him; I will not come.
  BOS: And what of this?

SCENE FIVE          MODERN

live more happily than we do, because they are free to choose their own lovers, and joyfully sing their happiness to the spring.

[*Enter* BOSOLA *with a letter*]

BOSOLA: It's fortunate I have caught up with you.
DUCHESS: This letter is from my brother?
BOSOLA: Yes, he sends it with all love and good faith.

DUCHESS: You are covering up danger/whitewashing it. See, just like the deceptive calm before a storm, deceptive people speak kindly to those they intend to harm. [*Reads.*] "*Send Antonio to me; I want his advice about a business matter.*" A crafty way of hiding of the truth! He doesn't want your advice; he wants your head. Meaning, he can't find peace until you, Antonio, are dead. And here's another trap that's disguised with nice-seeming words; pay attention to it, as it's a cunning one: [*Reads.*] "*I'm covering your husband's debt to the moneylenders in Naples, but that mustn't worry him. I want his heart* [figuratively friendship/love, but the Duchess realises the more literal meaning fits best] *more than his money.*" And I believe it.

BOSOLA: What do you believe?
DUCHESS: I believe he has so little faith in my husband's love for me that he will not trust the nature of my husband's heart until he sees it in the flesh. Ferdinand is a devil not clever enough to fool us with riddles.

BOSOLA: Are you rejecting the noble and free alliance of friendship and love which I present to you?

DUCHESS: Their alliance is like that of some scheming kings intending to make themselves stronger through ruining us — tell them so.
BOSOLA: And what message from you?
ANTONIO: Therefore tell them I will not come.
BOSOLA: And the reason for this?

135

ANT: My brothers have dispers'd
Bloodhounds abroad; which till I hear are muzzl'd,
No truce, though hatch'd with ne'er such politic skill,
50 Is safe, that hangs upon our enemies' will.
I 'll not come at them.
BOS: This proclaims your breeding.
Every small thing draws a base mind to fear,
As the adamant draws iron. Fare you well, sir;
You shall shortly hear from 's. [*Exit*.]
DUCH: I suspect some ambush;
55 Therefore by all my love I do conjure you
To take your eldest son, and fly towards Milan.
Let us not venture all this poor remainder
In one unlucky bottom.
ANT: You counsel safely.
Best of my life, farewell. Since we must part,
60 Heaven hath a hand in 't; but no otherwise
Than as some curious artist takes in sunder
A clock or watch, when it is out of frame,
To bring 't it in better order.
DUCH: I know not which is best,
To see you dead, or part with you.—Farewell, boy:
65 Thou art happy that thou hast not understanding
To know thy misery; for all our wit
And reading brings us to a truer sense
Of sorrow.—In the eternal church, sir,
I do hope we shall not part thus.
ANT: O, be of comfort!
70 Make patience a noble fortitude,
And think not how unkindly we are us'd:
Man, like to cassia, is prov'd best, being bruis'd.

DUCH: Must I, like to slave-born Russian,
Account it praise to suffer tyranny?
75 And yet, O heaven, thy heavy hand is in 't!
I have seen my little boy oft scourge his top,
And compar'd myself to 't: naught made me e'er

SCENE FIVE                MODERN

ANTONIO: My brothers (in law) have sent bloodhounds abroad to hunt me. Until I hear they have been restrained, no truce that depends on my enemies' good will is safe, no matter how cleverly it's presented. I'll not come to them.

BOSOLA: This is evidence of your lowly social status. Every tiny thing pulls a low-born mind into a state of fear, just as a magnet pulls iron. Farewell, sir. You'll hear from us soon. [*Exit.*]

DUCHESS: I suspect an ambush has been laid for us. Therefore, with all my love I implore you to take your eldest son and flee with him toward the city of Milan. It's best we split up, so that we don't risk all the little we have left in one basket.

ANTONIO: Sensible advice. Best thing in my life, goodbye. God has decided that we must part, but only in the same way a clockmaker takes apart a clock or watch, when it is telling the wrong time, so it may be put back together in better working order.

DUCHESS: I don't know whether I would rather see you dead or have to part from you. Farewell, boy: you're happy because you don't understand how truly miserable your situation is. People who have wisdom/knowledge/understanding feel more grief. [Possible allusion to Ecclesiastes: "he that increases knowledge increases sorrow".] I hope we won't be parted in heaven as we are now.

ANTONIO: Oh, cheer up! Think of the patience we must endure while we wait to be reunited as something that strengthens our minds. Don't dwell on how cruelly we're being treated. People are like spices, which release their full scent and flavour when beaten.

DUCHESS: Why should I think, as Russians born into slavery do, that it is praiseworthy to endure tyranny? And yet it is the oppressive will of heaven that I must endure it! I have often seen my little boy spinning his spinning-top by whipping it with a stick, and compared myself to it. Nothing ever guided me

ORIGINAL                                   ACT THREE

Go right but heaven's scourge-stick.

  ANT:    Do not weep.
Heaven fashion'd us of nothing; and we strive
80 To bring ourselves to nothing.—Farewell, Cariola,
And thy sweet armful.—If I do never see thee more,
Be a good mother to your little ones,
And save them from the tiger: fare you well.
    DUCH: Let me look upon you once more, for that speech
85 Came from a dying father. Your kiss is colder
Than that I have seen an holy anchorite
Give to a dead man's skull.
  ANT: My heart is turn'd to a heavy lump of lead,
With which I sound my danger: fare you well. [*Exeunt* ANTONIO *and his son.*]

---

### WHAT'S GOING ON?
*The Duchess is now well aware of Ferdinand's lethal intentions toward her family. As usual, she's the one who whips things together and comes up with a plan, while Antonio remains a somewhat passive passenger. She sends her son away with him, and keeps the other two children with her, to ensure that at least some of them will survive. All the doom and gloom, and talk of death,*

---

90   DUCH: My laurel is all withered.
  CARI: Look, madam, what a troop of armed men
Make toward us!
    [*Re-enter* BOSOLA *visarded, with a* Guard

  DUCH:    O, they are very welcome:
When Fortune's wheel is over-charg'd with princes,
The weight makes it move swift: I would have my ruin
95 Be sudden.—I am your adventure, am I not?

SCENE FIVE          MODERN

to do the right thing apart from the threat of God's
punishing whip [i.e. the threat of God's judgement].
ANTONIO: Don't cry. God created us out of nothing, and all
our struggles ultimately end by going back to nothing.
Farewell, Cariola, and my sweet children whom you hold in
your arms. [*To the* DUCHESS] If I never see you again, be a
good mother to your little ones, and save them from
danger. Farewell.
DUCHESS: Let me look at you one last time, because that
speech came from someone who thinks he is going to die.
Your kiss is colder than one an old religious hermit would
give to a dead man's skull.

ANTONIO: My heart is turned to a heavy lump of lead,
which I use to measure the depths of danger. [Nauticul
reference – sailors would dangle a lump of lead on a string
in the water to find out how deep it was.] Farewell.
    [*Exeunt* ANTONIO *with his son.*]

*does the familiar thing in tragedies of foreshadowing what's
to come.*

    *Bosola's trash talk about Antonio's social status is
interesting here, as it contrasts his earlier praise of Antonio's
worth earlier in the act. It keeps Bosola an enigmatic,
ambiguous character whose moral values are hard to precisely
pinpoint.*

DUCHESS: My happiness is withered away.
CARIOLA: Look, madam, at all these armed men coming
toward us!
    [*Re-enter* BOSOLA *masked/disguised, with a guard.
Due to Bosola's disguise, the Duchess doesn't recognise him in
the following section.*]
DUCHESS: Oh, I'm glad to see them. When there are too
many great people enjoying being on the top of the wheel
of fortune, the weight of them makes the wheel spin quickly
and their fortune soon turns bad. I would rather my ruin

139

BOS: You are: you must see your husband no more.
DUCH: What devil art thou that counterfeit'st heaven's thunder?

BOS: Is that terrible? I would have you tell me whether
Is that note worse that frights the silly birds
100 Out of the corn, or that which doth allure them
To the nets? You have heark'ned to the last too much.
DUCH: O misery! like to a rusty o'ercharg'd cannon,
Shall I never fly in pieces?—Come, to what prison?

BOS: To none.
DUCH: Whither, then?
BOS: To your palace.
105 DUCH: I have heard
That Charon's boat serves to convey all o'er
The dismal lake, but brings none back again.
BOS: Your brothers mean you safety and pity.

DUCH: Pity!
With such a pity men preserve alive
110 Pheasants and quails, when they are not fat enough
To be eaten.
BOS: These are your children?
DUCH: Yes.
BOS: Can they prattle?
DUCH: No.
But I intend, since they were born accurs'd,
Curses shall be their first language.
115 BOS: Fie, madam!
Forget this base, low fellow—
DUCH: Were I a man,
I'd beat that counterfeit face into thy other.
BOS: One of no birth.

comes quickly. [*To* BOSOLA] You've come for me, have you not?
BOSOLA: I have. You must not see your husband again.
DUCHESS: What devil are you that gives demands only God should give? [Marriage was considered a sacrament, meaning only God had the power to break one.]
BOSOLA: Is that bad? What's worse: the voice that frightens birds away, or the one that lures them into a trap? You have been lured by temptation too much, and now must pay the price.
DUCHESS: Oh, misery! Like a rusty old cannon that's charged with too much gunpowder and explodes, am I doomed to always be torn to pieces/to suffer? Tell me, to what prison are you taking me?
BOSOLA: To none.
DUCHESS: Where, then?
BOSOLA: To your palace.
DUCHESS: You bring to mind Charon, the mythological boatman who ferries souls across the river to the underworld, and never brings them back.
BOSOLA: Your brothers intend to show you only safety and pity.
DUCHESS: Pity?! Theirs is the sort of pity shown toward pheasants and quails who are killed because they're not fat enough to be eaten.

BOSOLA: These are your children?
DUCHESS: Yes.
BOSOLA: Can they talk?

DUCHESS: No. But because they were cursed when they were born [i.e. born into a cursed world/cursed circumstances] I intend for curses to be their first words.
BOSOLA: Enough, madam! Forget this crude, low-status Antonio —
DUCHESS: If I were a man I'd punch your fake, masked face into your real one.
BOSOLA: [finishing his interrupted comment] he is lowly born.

DUCH: Say that he was born mean,
Man is most happy when 's own actions
120 Be arguments and examples of his virtue.
  BOS: A barren, beggarly virtue.
  DUCH: I prithee, who is greatest? Can you tell?
Sad tales befit my woe: I 'll tell you one.
A salmon, as she swam unto the sea.
125 Met with a dog-fish, who encounters her
With this rough language; "Why art thou so bold
To mix thyself with our high state of floods,
Being no eminent courtier, but one
That for the calmest and fresh time o' th' year
130 Dost live in shallow rivers, rank'st thyself
With silly smelts and shrimps? And darest thou
Pass by our dog-ship without reverence?"
"O," quoth the salmon, "sister, be at peace:
Thank Jupiter we both have pass'd the net!
135 Our value never can be truly known,
Till in the fisher's basket we be shown:
I' th' market then my price may be the higher,
Even when I am nearest to the cook and fire."
So to great men the moral may be stretched;
140 Men oft are valu'd high, when they're most wretched.—
But come, whither you please. I am arm'd 'gainst misery;
Bent to all sways of the oppressor's will:
There 's no deep valley but near some great hill. [*Exeunt.*]

---

### WHAT'S GOING ON?
*Bosola, disguised, comes to take the Duchess back to the palace, where she will be confined by her brothers. The Duchess recognises that this is to be an imprisonment – and her reference to Charon suggests she realises she*

SCENE FIVE                MODERN

DUCHESS: So what if he was lowly born. The best man is one whose actions and behaviour show his value, not the status he was born into.
BOSOLA: Value without status is a barren, beggarly value.
DUCHESS: I ask you, do you know how to value people? Sad stories are fitting for my sad mood, so I'll tell you one. A salmon, swimming into the sea, meets a dog-fish, who greets her with this rough speech:
"Why are you so bold as to mix with our high-status breed of fish, being yourself just a lowly fish who, even in the calmest and freshest seasons, stays in shallow rivers among little fish and shrimp? And you dare pass by our dog-fish leader without showing respect?"

"Oh," said the salmon, "sister, be at peace — just be thankful we have both escaped the fishing net! Our value can never be truly known until we're lying dead in the fisherman's basket and a price is attached to us. In the market, then, my price might be higher than yours, even when I am nearest to the cook and fire."
So, the moral of the story is this: people are valued most highly when they are in their worst possible state. [The story perhaps serves to illustrate the fickleness of value judgements, or possibly how people have the most potential for "value" when suffering.] But come, take me where you want. I am prepared to fight against misery, being entirely subject to the power of my brothers' oppressive will. When things are really bad, they always get better soon, just as the lowest point of a valley soon turns uphill.       [*Exeunt.*]

*won't survive it. But she approaches the prospect with strength, threatening to punch Bosola in the face, and stays faithful to her moral values, defending Antonio against Bosola's jabs at his social status.*

ACT FOUR

Scene One

[Enter FERDINAND and BOSOLA]

FERD: How doth our sister duchess bear herself
In her imprisonment?
  BOS:      Nobly: I 'll describe her.
She 's sad as one long us'd to 't, and she seems
Rather to welcome the end of misery
5  Than shun it; a behaviour so noble
As gives a majesty to adversity:
You may discern the shape of loveliness
More perfect in her tears than in her smiles:
She will muse for hours together; and her silence,
10  Methinks, expresseth more than if she spake.
  FERD: Her melancholy seems to be fortified
With a strange disdain.
  BOS:      'Tis so; and this restraint,
Like English mastives that grow fierce with tying,
Makes her too passionately apprehend
Those pleasures she is kept from.
15  FERD:    Curse upon her!
I will no longer study in the book
Of another's heart. Inform her what I told you. [*Exit.*]

[*Enter* DUCHESS *and* Attendants]

  BOS: All comfort to your grace!
  DUCH:     I will have none.
Pray thee, why dost thou wrap thy poison'd pills
20  In gold and sugar?
  BOS: Your elder brother, the Lord Ferdinand,

SCENE ONE        MODERN

[*Enter* FERDINAND *and* BOSOLA — *the Duchess's palace.*]

FERDINAND: How is my sister Duchess coping with her imprisonment?
BOSOLA: In a noble way. I'll describe it: she appears sad in a way that suggests she's used to being sad, and she seems to look forward to death, as the end of her misery, rather than fearing it. Her behaviour is so noble that it makes her suffering seem majestic. She seems more beautiful in her sadness than when she's happy. She will sit in contemplation for four solid hours, and it is as if her silence communicates more than her speech.

FERDINAND: Her misery seems to be enriched by a strange bitterness.
BOSOLA: Yes, and this imprisonment makes her fiercely desire the family she is kept from, like dogs that grow fiercer when they're tied up.

FERDINAND: Damn her! I will no longer obsess myself with another person's thoughts and feelings. Tell her what I told you.    [*Exit.*]

[*Enter* DUCHESS *and* Attendants]

BOSOLA: I wish you all comfort.

DUCHESS: I don't want comfort. Tell me, why do you cover up your bad intentions toward me with this sweet politeness?
BOSOLA: Your elder brother [N.B. the Duchess and Ferdinand are in fact twins] Lord Ferdinand

Is come to visit you, and sends you word,
'Cause once he rashly made a solemn vow
Never to see you more, he comes i' th' night;
25 And prays you gently neither torch nor taper
Shine in your chamber. He will kiss your hand,
And reconcile himself; but for his vow
He dares not see you.
  DUCH:   At his pleasure.—
Take hence the lights.—He 's come.  [*Exeunt* Attendants
*with lights.*]

  [*Enter* FERDINAND]

  FERD:   Where are you?
  DUCH:   Here, sir.
  FERD:  This darkness suits you well.
30   DUCH:   I would ask your pardon.
  FERD:  You have it;
For I account it the honorabl'st revenge,
Where I may kill, to pardon.—Where are your cubs?
  DUCH:  Whom?
35   FERD:   Call them your children;
For though our national law distinguish bastards
From true legitimate issue, compassionate nature
Makes them all equal.
  DUCH:   Do you visit me for this?
You violate a sacrament o' th' church
Shall make you howl in hell for 't.
40   FERD:   It had been well,
Could you have liv'd thus always; for, indeed,
You were too much i' th' light:—but no more;
I come to seal my peace with you. Here 's a hand  [Gives
her a dead man's hand.]
To which you have vow'd much love; the ring upon 't
You gave.
45   DUCH:   I affectionately kiss it.

146

has come to visit you, and wants you to know that because he once made a vow never to see you again, he will come in darkness, and asks you not to shine any light in your chamber. He will kiss your hand, and be friendly to you, but because of this vow he dares not to see you.

DUCHESS: Whatever he wants. Then take the lights away — he's coming. [*Exeunt* Attendants *with lights — stage is now totally dark.*]

   [*Enter* FERDINAND]

FERDINAND: Where are you?
DUCHESS: Here, sir.
FERDINAND: Darkness suits an immoral person like you.
DUCHESS: I want to ask for your forgiveness.
FERDINAND: You have it. I think it is the most honourable form of revenge, to give forgiveness when I have the power to kill. Where are your cubs?
DUCHESS: Who do you mean?
FERDINAND: Call them your children, because although by law they are considered illegitimate bastards not born from a legitimate marriage, compassionate nature considers all children equal.
DUCHESS: Is this why you've come here, to insult my family? Your disregard of my marriage's legitimacy is a violation against God who brought my husband and me together. You'll howl in hell as punishment.
FERDINAND: It would have been better if you'd always lived in the dark like this, because too much of your life was spent exposed to the light of public eyes. But we'll say no more about this. I have come to make peace with you. Here's a hand. [*He offers her a dead man's hand — being in the dark, she thinks it is Ferdinand's own hand.*] You've promised much love to this hand, and you gave the ring worn by it.
DUCHESS: I affectionately kiss it.

FERD:  Pray, do, and bury the print of it in your heart.
I will leave this ring with you for a love-token;
And the hand as sure as the ring; and do not doubt
But you shall have the heart too. When you need a friend,
50 Send it to him that ow'd it; you shall see
Whether he can aid you.

DUCH:    You are very cold:
I fear you are not well after your travel.—
Ha! lights!—O, horrible!
    FERD:    Let her have lights enough.  [*Exit.*]
    [*Enter* Servants *with lights.*]
    DUCH:  What witchcraft doth he practise, that he hath left
55 A dead man's hand here? [Here is discovered, behind a traverse, the artificial figures of ANTONIO and his children, appearing as if they were dead.
    BOS:  Look you, here's the piece from which 'twas ta'en.
He doth present you this sad spectacle,
That, now you know directly they are dead,
Hereafter you may wisely cease to grieve
60 For that which cannot be recovered.
    DUCH:  There is not between heaven and earth one wish
I stay for after this. It wastes me more
Than were 't my picture, fashion'd out of wax,
Stuck with a magical needle, and then buried
65 In some foul dunghill; and yon's an excellent property
For a tyrant, which I would account mercy.
    BOS:    What's that?
    DUCH:  If they would bind me to that lifeless trunk,
And let me freeze to death.
    BOS:    Come, you must live.
70  DUCH:  That's the greatest torture souls feel in hell,
In hell, that they must live, and cannot die.

SCENE ONE                    MODERN

FERDINAND: Please do, with all your heart. I will leave the ring with you as a reminder of my love, and the hand as well as the ring, and don't doubt that you have the heart too. When you need a friend, call for the person who owned it, and you'll see whether he can help you or not. [The Duchess presumably doesn't yet realise the double-meaning of Ferdinand's speech – he could be referring to Antonio as well as himself here.]

DUCHESS: Your hand feels very cold. I worry you're not well after your long journey. Oh! Bring lights! Oh, how horrible! [She realises she's kissed a dead hand.]

FERDINAND: Let her have plenty of lights. [*Exit.*]

  [*Enter* Servants *with lights.*]

DUCHESS: What sort of witchcraft has used to conjure a dead man's hand? [*A panel at the back of the stage slides back to reveal what looks like the figures of* ANTONIO *and the children, dead. They are artificial – but the Duchess doesn't know this.*]

BOSOLA: Look – here's the body from which that hand was taken. Ferdinand presents this sad sight to you so that you will know they are certainly dead and so that you won't grieve for long, which will be wise, because there's no use grieving something that can't be recovered.

DUCHESS: There is nothing between heaven and earth I want to stay alive for after seeing this. It hurts me more than if I were seeing myself, fashioned out of wax and stabbed with a magical needle, then buried in a heap of dung. There is an excellent sort of thing a tyrant would do which I would consider a mercy.

BOSOLA: What's that?
DUCHESS: Tie me to that lifeless body of my husband and let me freeze to death.
BOSOLA: Come, you must live.
DUCHESS: That's the greatest torture felt by souls in hell, that they must live, enduring agony, and cannot die.

Portia, I'll new kindle thy coals again,
And revive the rare and almost dead example
Of a loving wife.
  BOS:     O, fie! despair? Remember
You are a Christian.
75   DUCH:    The church enjoins fasting:
I'll starve myself to death.
  BOS:     Leave this vain sorrow.
Things being at the worst begin to mend: the bee
When he hath shot his sting into your hand,
May then play with your eye-lid.
  DUCH:    Good comfortable fellow,
80  Persuade a wretch that's broke upon the wheel
To have all his bones new set; entreat him live
To be executed again. Who must despatch me?
I account this world a tedious theatre,
For I do play a part in 't 'gainst my will.

85  BOS: Come, be of comfort; I will save your life.
  DUCH: Indeed, I have not leisure to tend so small a business.
  BOS: Now, by my life, I pity you.
  DUCH:    Thou art a fool, then,
To waste thy pity on a thing so wretched
As cannot pity itself. I am full of daggers.
90  Puff, let me blow these vipers from me.
    [*Enter* Servant]
What are you?
  SERV.    One that wishes you long life.
  DUCH: I would thou wert hang'd for the horrible curse
Thou hast given me: I shall shortly grow one
Of the miracles of pity. I'll go pray;— [*Exit* Servant.]
No, I'll go curse.
  BOS:    O, fie!
95  DUCH:    I could curse the stars.
  BOS:    O, fearful!

SCENE ONE　　　　　　　MODERN

Brutus' wife Portia killed herself by swallowing hot coals, and I will do the same, to be a rare example of a truly loving wife.

BOSOLA: Oh come on, what is this despair? Remember you are a Christian, therefore suicide is a sin.

DUCHESS: Christianity encourages fasting, so I'll starve myself to death.

BOSOLA: Leave this useless sorrow. Now things are at their worst, they can only get better. When the bee has shot all its sting into your hand, it's no longer a threat.

DUCHESS: Good comfortable fellow, asking me to go on living is like asking a poor wretch who's been tortured by being tied to a wheel and having his bones broken to have his bones fixed so he can go through the same torture again. Who is going to kill me? I think of this world as a tedious play in a theatre, and I play my part in it against my will.

BOSOLA: Come, be comforted; I will save your life.

DUCHESS: Indeed, I don't have any interest in tending to such unimportant business as saving my life myself.

BOSOLA: Now, I swear on my life, I feel sorry for you.

DUCHESS: Then you're a fool to waste pity on a thing so wretched it's unable to feel pity for itself. I have been hurt so badly I am close to dying, full of daggers like the sting of snakes – puff, let me blow them away from me.

　　　[*Enter* Servant]

Who are you?

SERVANT: Someone who wishes you a long life.

DUCHESS: I'd like to have you hanged as punishment for the cruelty of wishing me long life. I will soon become an object of enormous pity for anyone who looks at me. I will go and pray – [*Exit* Servant] – no, I'll go curse.

BOSOLA: Oh, enough of this!

DUCHESS: I could curse the stars that have brought this fate upon me.

BOSOLA: Oh, how formidable!

DUCH: And those three smiling seasons of the year
Into a Russian winter; nay, the world
To its first chaos.
   BOS:   Look you, the stars shine still.

   DUCH: O, but you must
100 Remember, my curse hath a great way to go.—
Plagues, that make lanes through largest families,
Consume them!—
   BOS:   Fie, lady!
   DUCH:   Let them, like tyrants,
Never be remembered but for the ill they have done;
Let all the zealous prayers of mortified
Churchmen forget them!—
105 BOS:   O, uncharitable!
   DUCH: Let heaven a little while cease crowning martyrs,
To punish them!—
Go, howl them this, and say, I long to bleed:
It is some mercy when men kill with speed. [*Exit.*]

   [*Re-enter* FERDINAND]

110 FERD: Excellent, as I would wish; she 's plagu'd in art.
These presentations are but fram'd in wax
By the curious master in that quality,
Vincentio Lauriola, and she takes them
For true substantial bodies.
   BOS:   Why do you do this?
   FERD: To bring her to despair.

115 BOS:   Faith, end here,
And go no farther in your cruelty:
Send her a penitential garment to put on
Next to her delicate skin, and furnish her
With beads and prayer-books.
   FERD:   Damn her! that body of hers.

SCENE ONE                              MODERN

DUCHESS: And I'll curse the three nice seasons of the year into a terrible winter; no, I'll curse the world into its state of chaos before it was created.
BOSOLA: Look — the stars are still shining despite your curse against them.
DUCHESS: Oh, but you must remember, my curse will take a long time to cause its destruction, just like plagues that slowly carve their way through great families and eventually consume them!

BOSOLA: Stop, lady!

DUCHESS: Let my brothers be remembered only for the terrible things they have done. Let them never be thought of in all the energetic prayers of really religious people!

BOSOLA: How unkind!
DUCHESS: Let heaven stop making saints, to punish my brothers! Go and howl this to them: tell my brothers I want to bleed; I want to die. It would be merciful to kill me quickly. [*Exit.*]


[*Re-enter* FERDINAND]


FERDINAND: How wonderful! Just as I wanted — she's been totally fooled by my fake props. These dead bodies of her husband and children are just wax models, made by the master of wax models, Vincentio Lauriola, and she thinks they're real!
BOSOLA: Why are you doing this?
FERDINAND: To bring her to despair [implying "to bring her to my state of despair / to share my despair].
BOSOLA: For God's sake stop. Stop your cruelty. Send her the sort of clothing a Catholic monk would wear, with beads and prayer-books, so she can seek forgiveness from God.


FERDINAND: Damn her and that body of hers to hell!

> 120 While that my blood run pure in 't, was more worth
> Than that which thou wouldst comfort, call'd a soul.
> I will send her masques of common courtezans,
> Have her meat serv'd up by bawds and ruffians,
> And, 'cause she 'll needs be mad, I am resolv'd
> 125 To move forth the common hospital
> All the mad-folk, and place them near her lodging;
> There let them practise together, sing and dance,
> And act their gambols to the full o' th' moon:
> If she can sleep the better for it, let her.
> Your work is almost ended.

> 130 BOS: Must I see her again?
> FERD: Yes.
> BOS: Never.
> FERD: You must.
> BOS: Never in mine own shape;
> That 's forfeited by my intelligence
> And this last cruel lie: when you send me next,
> The business shall be comfort.

> FERD: Very likely.
> 135 Thy pity is nothing of kin to thee. Antonio
> Lurks about Milan: thou shalt shortly thither,
> To feed a fire as great as my revenge,
> Which nev'r will slack till it hath spent his fuel:
> Intemperate agues make physicians cruel.  [*Exeunt.*]

---

### WHAT'S GOING ON?

*While holding the Duchess captive in her own palace, Ferdinand tortures her by tricking her into kissing a dead man's hand and then revealing the figures of Antonio and her son, murdered. The Duchess doesn't know that these are just wax figures. Her reaction ranges between fury, nihilism, and senility, but her wish to die is the most prominent thrust of it.*

*Ferdinand's tortures are externalisations of his own*

SCENE ONE  MODERN

While my blood ran pure in it (before it was corrupted with Antonio's), her body was worth more than her soul, which people like you believe exists, and which you try to comfort. I'm going to arrange a party for her, where the musicians and dancers will be prostitutes. The meat will be her body, served up by pimps and scumbags, and, because I need to make her insane, I have decided to move all the mad people from the local asylum and put them near her lodging. There they and the Duchess can practise being mad together, singing and dancing and gambolling for the full moon, when mad people are at their worst. If by any slim chance she manages to sleep through all that, then let her. Your work is almost over.
BOSOLA: Must I see her again?
FERDINAND: Yes.
BOSOLA: I flatly refuse.
FERDINAND: You must.
BOSOLA: Not without a disguise, because now she knows I had a role in her demise and these last terrible tricks played on her, and I feel too guilty to show her my own face. When you send me to her next, it will be to give her comfort.
FERDINAND: Very likely, but your pity doesn't suit you well. Antonio is lurking about in Milan. You'll go there soon to exact my revenge, which is like a great fire, and my need for revenge won't die until everything that fuels it has gone. It is like a disease, and to cure it the doctor must take desperate measures.   [*Exeunt.*]

---

*perverse desires — his jealousy demands the elimination of those the Duchess loves, and his attack on her mental state is a means of making her share his own internal despair. His actions continue to be governed by "need" rather than by calculating logic.*

*Bosola seems to be undergoing a sort of moral awakening, and now feels so guilty for his involvement in the Duchess's downfall that he refuses to show his face to her again, and will only see her when he's disguised.*

## Act Four

Scene Two

*[Enter DUCHESS and CARIOLA]*

DUCH: What hideous noise was that?
CARI: 'Tis the wild consort
Of madmen, lady, which your tyrant brother
Hath plac'd about your lodging. This tyranny,
I think, was never practis'd till this hour.
5   DUCH: Indeed, I thank him. Nothing but noise and folly
Can keep me in my right wits; whereas reason
And silence make me stark mad. Sit down;
Discourse to me some dismal tragedy.
CARI: O, 'twill increase your melancholy!
DUCH: Thou art deceiv'd:
10  To hear of greater grief would lessen mine,
This is a prison?
CARI: Yes, but you shall live
To shake this durance off.
DUCH: Thou art a fool:
The robin-red-breast and the nightingale
Never live long in cages.
CARI: Pray, dry your eyes.
15  What think you of, madam?
DUCH: Of nothing;
When I muse thus, I sleep.
CARI: Like a madman, with your eyes open?
DUCH: Dost thou think we shall know one another
In th' other world?
20  CARI: Yes, out of question.

SCENE TWO	MODERN

[*Enter* DUCHESS *and* CARIOLA.]

DUCHESS: What is that hideous noise?
CARIOLA: It's the mad band of musicians which your tyrant brother has positioned around your rooms, my lady. Such tyranny as this has never been done before now.

DUCHESS: I'm grateful for it, because only the distraction of noise and foolishness can keep me sane, whereas rationality and silence will send me mad. Sit down; tell me a story about some terrible tragedy.

CARIOLA: Oh, that will just make your sadness worse!
DUCHESS: You're wrong. To hear about a greater grief would make mine feel not so bad. Am I in a prison?

CARIOLA: Yes, but you will live through these tough times.

DUCHESS: You're a fool. Like the robin-red-breast and the nightingale, people like me can't live for long in cages.

CARIOLA: Please, dry your tears. What are you thinking about, madam?
DUCHESS: About nothing. When I think of nothing, I can sleep.
CARIOLA: Like a madman, with your eyes open?
DUCHESS: Do you think we'll be together in the afterlife?

CARIOLA: Without a doubt.

DUCH: O, that it were possible we might
But hold some two days' conference with the dead!
From them I should learn somewhat, I am sure,
I never shall know here. I 'll tell thee a miracle:
25 I am not mad yet, to my cause of sorrow;
Th' heaven o'er my head seems made of molten brass,
The earth of flaming sulphur, yet I am not mad.
I am acquainted with sad misery
As the tann'd galley-slave is with his oar;
30 Necessity makes me suffer constantly,
And custom makes it easy. Who do I look like now?
  CARI: Like to your picture in the gallery,
A deal of life in show, but none in practice;
Or rather like some reverend monument
Whose ruins are even pitied.
35   DUCH:     Very proper:
And Fortune seems only to have her eye-sight
To behold my tragedy.—How now!
What noise is that?
   [*Enter* Servant]
  SERV.     I am come to tell you
Your brother hath intended you some sport,
40 A great physician, when the Pope was sick
Of a deep melancholy, presented him
With several sorts of madmen, which wild object
Being full of change and sport, forc'd him to laugh,
And so the imposthume broke: the self-same cure
The duke intends on you.
45   DUCH:     Let them come in.
  SERV. There 's a mad lawyer; and a secular priest;
A doctor that hath forfeited his wits
By jealousy; an astrologian
That in his works said such a day o' the month
50 Should be the day of doom, and, failing of 't,
Ran mad; an English tailor craz'd i' the brain
With the study of new fashions; a gentleman-usher
Quite beside himself with care to keep in mind

SCENE TWO                    MODERN

DUCHESS: Oh, if only it were possible to spend a couple of days talking to dead people! From them I could learn things I'll never learn from the living. I'll tell you something miraculous: I'm not mad yet — and this makes me sad. Both the heaven above and the earth below seem places of terrible punishment, and yet I am not mad. I have known misery for a long time, just like the galley slave has long known the oar. It is a necessity for me to constantly suffer, and it's easy because suffering has become a habit. Who do I look like now?

CARIOLA: You look like your portrait that hangs in the gallery, appearing on the surface to be full of life, but not really having any. Or you look like some ancient respected monument who people pity because it is ruined.

DUCHESS: Very appropriate. And Fortune, normally blind, now has eyesight, so keen it is to observe my tragic circumstances. What's this? What is that noise?

[*Enter* Servant]

SERVANT: I am here to tell you your brother has arranged some entertainment for you. A great doctor once presented the Pope, when he was sick with depression, with a variety of mad people, which forced the Pope to laugh, and broke the ulcer of his sickness. Ferdinand intends to give you the same cure.

DUCHESS: Let them come in.

SERVANT: There's a mad lawyer; and a non-religious priest; a doctor sent mad by jealousy; an astrologer who predicted the day of doom and went mad when it didn't happen; an English tailor whose studies of the latest fashions have made him crazy in the brain; a gentleman-usher, who attends ladies at parties and functions, and went mad trying to remember all the ways the ladies liked to be greeted;

The number of his lady's salutations
55 Or 'How do you,' she employ'd him in each morning;
A farmer, too, an excellent knave in grain,
Mad 'cause he was hind'red transportation:
And let one broker that 's mad loose to these,
You'd think the devil were among them.

60    DUCH: Sit, Cariola.—Let them loose when you please,
For I am chain'd to endure all your tyranny.

   [*Enter* Madman]
   *Here by a Madman this song is sung to a dismal kind of music*

>*O, let us howl some heavy note,*
>  *Some deadly dogged howl,*
>*Sounding as from the threatening throat*
65   *Of beasts and fatal fowl!*
>*As ravens, screech-owls, bulls, and bears,*
>  *We 'll bell, and bawl our parts,*
>*Till irksome noise have cloy'd your ears*
>  *And corrosiv'd your hearts.*
70 *At last, when as our choir wants breath,*
>  *Our bodies being blest,*
>*We 'll sing, like swans, to welcome death,*
>  *And die in love and rest.*

   MAD ASTROLOGER. Doom's-day not come yet? I'll
75 draw it nearer by a perspective, or make a glass that shall
set all the world on fire upon an instant. I cannot sleep;
my pillow is stuffed with a litter of porcupines.

   MAD LAWYER. Hell is a mere glass-house, where the
devils are continually blowing up women's souls on
80 hollow irons, and the fire never goes out.

SCENE TWO                MODERN

a farmer who profited by being dishonest in his deals with grain and went mad because he was stopped from transporting his grain to market. If you let loose among them one broker — someone who serves as a middleman in business negotiations, and is therefore well placed for causing chaos — you'd witness the sort of chaos that would make you think the devil had come among them.
DUCHESS: Sit, Cariola. [*To the* Servant] Let them loose whenever you want, for I have no choice but to endure all your tyranny.

[*Enter* Madman]

*The following, largely nonsensical, song is sung by one of the madmen to a dismal tune.*

*Oh, let us howl miserable music,*
*Some deadly wolf-like howl,*
*Sounding as if it comes from the threatening throats*
*Of beasts and birds of prey!*
*Like ravens, screech-owls, bulls, and bears,*
*We'll bellow, and cry out our song,*
*Until annoying noise has sickened your ears*
*And corroded your heart.*
*At last, when our singers have run out of breath,*
*Our bodies being blessed,*
*We'll sing, like swans, to welcome death,*
*And die in love and peace.*

MAD ASTROLOGER: Hasn't the world ended yet? I'll make the end come closer by looking at it through a telescope, or by making a magnifying glass that will instantly set the whole world on fire. I can't sleep because my pillow is stuffed full of porcupines.

MAD LAWYER: Hell is just a glass factory, where the devils are always blowing up women's souls on hollow irons (in the same way glassblowing is done) and the fire never goes out.

MAD PRIEST: I will lie with every woman in my parish the tenth night; I will tithe them over like haycocks.

MAD DOCTOR: Shall my 'pothecary outgo me, because I am a cuckold? I have found out his roguery; he makes
85 alum of his wife's urine, and sells it to Puritans that have sore throats with overstraining.

MAD ASTROLOGER. I have skill in heraldry.

MAD LAWYER. Hast?
MAD ASTROLOGER. You do give for your crest a
90 woodcock's head with the brains picked out on 't; you are a very ancient gentleman.
MAD PRIEST. Greek is turned Turk: we are only to be saved by the Helvetian translation.

MAD ASTROLOGER. Come on, sir, I will lay the law
95 to you.
MAD LAWYER. O, rather lay a corrosive: the law will eat to the bone.
MAD PRIEST. He that drinks but to satisfy nature is damn'd.
MAD DOCTOR. If I had my glass here, I would show a sight should make all the women here call me mad
100 doctor.
MAD ASTROLOGER. What 's he? a rope-maker?

MAD LAWYER. No, no, no, a snuffling knave that, while he shows the tombs, will have his hand in a wench's placket.
105 MAD PRIEST. Woe to the caroche that brought home my wife from the masque at three o'clock in the morning! It had a large feather-bed in it.
MAD DOCTOR. I have pared the devil's nails forty times, roasted them in raven's eggs, and cured agues with them.

SCENE TWO        MODERN

MAD PRIEST: I will collect the church's tax payment from the people by sleeping with every woman in my parish every tenth night, like farmers pay taxes with their hay.

MAD DOCTOR: Is my pharmacist outdoing me because my wife's cheating on me? He makes more money because his wife gives him her urine which he makes into an ointment. He sells it to Puritans who have sore throats from preaching so loudly.

MAD ASTROLOGER: I have some knowledge about designing coats of arms.

MAD LAWYER: Oh, have you?

MAD ASTROLOGER: If you put on your crest the head of the foolish woodcock bird, with all its brains picked out, then you show yourself to be a gentleman of high pedigree.

MAD PRIEST: The holy Greek language of the Bible has been turned heathen in modern translation; only the Helvetian translation can restore it.

MAD ASTROLOGER: Come on sir, I will tell you about the law.

MAD LAWYER: The law is more capable of eating away your flesh than an acid.

MAD PRIEST: He that drinks only as much as he needs to survive is damned — drunkards are blessed.

MAD DOCTOR: If I had my mirror, I could show you a sight that would make all the women here call me a mad doctor.

MAD ASTROLOGER: Who's he? Does he make rope for the hangman?

MAD LAWYER: No, no, no, he's just a scoundrel who will have his hands in a prostitute's petticoat while he gives people tours around a graveyard.

MAD PRIEST: Woe to the carriage that brought my wife home from the party at three o'clock in the morning! It had a large feather bed in it (used for sexual engagements).

MAD DOCTOR: I have trimmed the devil's fingernails forty times, roasted them in ravens' eggs, and cured diseases with them.

110   MAD PRIEST.  Get me three hundred milch-bats, to make possets to procure sleep.

MAD DOCTOR.  All the college may throw their caps at me: I have made a soap-boiler costive; it was my masterpiece. *Here the dance, consisting of Eight Madmen, with music answerable thereunto.*

---

### WHAT'S GOING ON?
*To make his sister feel his own despair, Ferdinand surrounds her with mad people. But their nonsensical song and ramblings don't have the effect on the Duchess that Ferdinand had hoped for. Rather than making her insane, she instead welcomes the peace they*

---

[*Enter* BOSOLA, *like an old man.*]

DUCH: Is he mad too?
SERV.   Pray, question him. I'll leave you. [*Exeunt* Servant *and* Madmen.]
BOS: I am come to make thy tomb.
115 DUCH:   Ha! my tomb!
Thou speak'st as if I lay upon my death-bed,
Gasping for breath. Dost thou perceive me sick?
BOS: Yes, and the more dangerously, since thy sickness is insensible.
120 DUCH: Thou art not mad, sure: dost know me?
BOS:   Yes.
DUCH:   Who am I?
BOS: Thou art a box of worm-seed, at best but a salvatory of green mummy. What's this flesh? a little
125 crudded milk, fantastical puff-paste. Our bodies are weaker than those paper-prisons boys use to keep flies in; more contemptible, since ours is to preserve earth-worms. Didst thou ever see a lark in a cage? Such is the soul in the body: this world is like her little turf of grass, and the
130 heaven o'er our heads like her looking-glass, only gives us

SCENE TWO    MODERN

MAD PRIEST: Get me three-hundred bats (of the flying kind) to make hot drinks for bringing on sleep.
MAD DOCTOR: Let the medical colleges try and stop me, but I have found a way to make even a soap-maker (known for having diarrhoea) constipated. It is my masterpiece.
[*Here begins a dance, consisting of eight madmen and appropriately mad music.*]

---

*bring by distracting her from her own torturous thoughts. Even in this desperate situation, the Duchess has the strength to subvert her brothers' oppressive attempts to control her.*

---

[*When the madmen's dance is finished, BOSOLA enters, disguised as an old man so the Duchess doesn't recognise him.*]
DUCHESS: Is he mad too?
SERVANT: Please, ask him yourself. I'll leave you. [*Exeunt* Servant *and* Madmen.]
BOSOLA: I am here to make your tomb.
DUCHESS: Ha! My tomb? You speak as if I'm on the verge of death, gasping for breath. Do I look sick to you?

BOSOLA: Yes, you do, and dangerously sick, because your sickness isn't a physical one.
DUCHESS: You don't seem mad. Do you know me?
BOSOLA: Yes.
DUCHESS: Who am I?

BOSOLA: You're a box of dirt, at best a container for the drug said to ooze from mummified bodies. What is flesh? Nothing but curdled milk, or light, insubstantial pastry. Our bodies are weaker than the paper traps boys make for flies; and less worthy, since our bodies end up just being containers for earth-worms. The soul in the human body is like a lark in a cage — this world is her little bit of grass, and the heavens over our heads are like her mirror, only a miserable knowledge of the small compass of our prison.

DUCH: Am not I thy duchess?

BOS: Thou art some great woman, sure, for riot begins to sit on thy forehead (clad in gray hairs) twenty years
sooner than on a merry milk-maid's. Thou sleepest worse than if a mouse should be forced to take up her lodging in a cat's ear: a little infant that breeds its teeth, should it lie with thee, would cry out, as if thou wert the more unquiet bedfellow.

DUCH: I am Duchess of Malfi still.

BOS: That makes thy sleep so broken:
Glories, like glow-worms, afar off shine bright,
But, look'd to near, have neither heat nor light.

DUCH: Thou art very plain.

BOS: My trade is to flatter the dead, not the living; I am a tomb-maker.

DUCH: And thou comest to make my tomb?

BOS: Yes.

DUCH: Let me be a little merry:—of what stuff wilt thou make it?

BOS: Nay, resolve me first, of what fashion?

DUCH: Why, do we grow fantastical on our deathbed? Do we affect fashion in the grave?

BOS: Most ambitiously. Princes' images on their tombs do not lie, as they were wont, seeming to pray up to heaven; but with their hands under their cheeks, as if they died of the tooth-ache. They are not carved with their eyes fix'd upon the stars, but as their minds were wholly bent upon the world, the selfsame way they seem to turn their faces.

showing us the miserable knowledge of the small boundaries of our prison.

DUCHESS: Am I not your Duchess?

BOSOLA: You're certainly some great woman, because beneath your grey hair your face is getting wrinkled twenty years sooner than a merry milk-maid's would. You are so troubled you sleep worse than a mouse if it were forced to rest in a cat's ear. A little infant with teething pain would cry out if it were resting with you, as if you were more restless than it.

DUCHESS: I am still the Duchess of Malfi.

BOSOLA: And that is why your sleep is so disturbed. The glories of princely rulers like you look magnificent from a distance, but turn out to be hollow when you look at them closely.

DUCHESS: You speak in a very unflattering way.

BOSOLA: My trade is to flatter the dead by making them ready for their graves [Bosola is posing as an undertaker], not to flatter the living.

DUCHESS: And you've come to make my tomb?

BOSOLA: Yes.

DUCHESS: Let me have a bit of fun with this — of what material will you make it?

BOSOLA: No, tell me first, what style of appearance do you want it to have?

DUCHESS: Why? Do you think we're prone to extravagance on our deathbed? Do we worry about style when we're dead?

BOSOLA: We certainly do. Princes' statues in their tombs no longer lie on their backs as if they're praying up to heaven, as the style used to be, but instead they have their hands under their cheeks, as if they died of the toothache. Their statues are not carved with their eyes fixed on the heavens and God, but as if their minds were completely fixated on the material world, just as their faces are turned toward it.

ORIGINAL  ACT FOUR

### WHAT'S GOING ON?
*Bosola said to Ferdinand in the previous scene that he would only see the Duchess again to comfort her. He's got a pretty odd way of doing this, but for someone not used to comforting people, it's perhaps not a bad attempt. He comes disguised as a tomb-maker — an undertaker, who prepares bodies for funerals. His*

---

160    DUCH: Let me know fully therefore the effect
Of this thy dismal preparation,
This talk fit for a charnel.
    BOS:     Now I shall:—
    [*Enter* Executioners, *with a coffin, cords, and a bell*]
Here is a present from your princely brothers;
And may it arrive welcome, for it brings
Last benefit, last sorrow.
165    DUCH:     Let me see it:
I have so much obedience in my blood,
I wish it in their veins to do them good.
    BOS: This is your last presence-chamber.

    CARI: O my sweet lady!
    DUCH:     Peace; it affrights not me.
170    BOS: I am the common bellman
That usually is sent to condemn'd persons
The night before they suffer.
    DUCH:     Even now thou said'st
Thou wast a tomb-maker.
    BOS:     'Twas to bring you
By degrees to mortification. Listen.
175         *Hark, now everything is still,*
        *The screech-owl and the whistler shrill*
        *Call upon our dame aloud,*

SCENE TWO                    MODERN

*comfort comes in preparing her for death stressing how earth
and human nature is corrupt, how her ties to the world —
particularly her status as Duchess — are causes of turmoil from
which she would best be freed.*
*Contrary to Ferdinand's intentions, the Duchess's mind isn't
being beaten. In fact she shows increasing composure,
appearing more collected and stoic now than in the previous
scene.*

---

DUCHESS: Let me know fully what this is all leading up to,
this dismal preparation of yours, this talk fit for a crypt.

BOSOLA: Now I will —
    [*Enter* Executioners, *with a coffin, ropes, and a bell*]
Here is a present from your princely brothers, and may you
be glad to see it, for it is the last good thing for you, and
the final sorrow you must endure.
DUCHESS: Let me see it: My blood is so full of obedience
and goodness, I wish it could run through their veins instead
of their impure, bad blood.

BOSOLA: [Probably gesturing toward the coffin] This is your
last presence-chamber [the place in a palace where a
sovereign such as the Duchess would have carried out
political business].
CARIOLA: Oh, my sweet lady!
DUCHESS: Hush; it doesn't frighten me.
BOSOLA: I am the common bellman (conventionally sent to
scare away evil spirits before someone's soul departs for
heaven).
DUCHESS: You said just now you were here only to make
my tomb, not to kill me.
BOSOLA: I said that to prepare you gently for your death.
Listen:
*Hear, now everything is still,*
*The screech-owl and the whistling bird, both signs of bad luck,*
*Sing to our Duchess loudly,*

*And bid her quickly don her shroud!*

*Much you had of land and rent;*
*Your length in clay 's now competent:*

*A long war disturb'd your mind;*
*Here your perfect peace is sign'd.*
*Of what is 't fools make such vain keeping?*
*Sin their conception, their birth weeping,*
*Their life a general mist of error,*
*Their death a hideous storm of terror.*
*Strew your hair with powders sweet,*
*Don clean linen, bathe your feet,*
*And (the foul fiend more to check)*
*A crucifix let bless your neck.*
*'Tis now full tide 'tween night and day;*
*End your groan, and come away.*

[EXECUTIONERS *approach.*]
CARI: Hence, villains, tyrants, murderers! Alas! What will you do with my lady?—Call for help!
DUCH: To whom? To our next neighbours? They are mad-folks.
BOS: Remove that noise.

DUCH: Farewell, Cariola.
In my last will I have not much to give:
A many hungry guests have fed upon me;
Thine will be a poor reversion.
CARI: I will die with her.
DUCH: I pray thee, look thou giv'st my little boy
Some syrup for his cold, and let the girl
Say her prayers ere she sleep. [CARIOLA *is forced out by the* Executioners.]
Now what you please:
What death?
BOS: Strangling; here are your executioners.

SCENE TWO        MODERN

*And ask her to quickly put on the sheet that will wrap her corpse!*
*You had plenty of material wealth,*
*But now all you need is enough space for your body to be dug into clay.*
*A long war disturbed your mind;*
*Here your perfect peace is promised.*
*Why are fools so obsessed with this material world?*
*They are brought into this world through a sinful act and emerge into it crying,*
*Their life is full of mistakes,*
*Their death is a hideous terror.*
*Powder your hair with sweet perfume*
*And wear clean linen, bathe your feet,*
*And (to keep away the devil)*
*Wear a crucifix around your neck.*
*It's now midnight:*
*End your suffering by dying.*

   [EXECUTIONERS *approach.*]

CARIOLA: Get out of here you villains, you murderers! What are you going to do to my lady? Call for help!

DUCHESS: To whom? Our neighbours? They are all mad people.

BOSOLA: [Gesturing toward Cariola and speaking to executioners] Get that noise out of here.

DUCHESS: Farewell, Cariola. I don't have much to give you in my will. Everything has been taken from me by many hungry people. You won't inherit much from me.

CARIOLA: I will die with her.

DUCHESS: Please Cariola, look after my children – give my little boy syrup when he has a cold, and let my little girl say her prayers before she goes to sleep. [CARIOLA *is forced out by the executioners.*] Now, what way do you want to kill me?

BOSOLA: Strangling. Here are your executioners.

DUCH: I forgive them:
205 The apoplexy, catarrh, or cough o' th' lungs,
Would do as much as they do.
 BOS: Doth not death fright you?
 DUCH: Who would be afraid on 't,
Knowing to meet such excellent company
In th' other world?
 BOS: Yet, methinks,
210 The manner of your death should much afflict you:
This cord should terrify you.
 DUCH: Not a whit:
What would it pleasure me to have my throat cut
With diamonds? or to be smothered
With cassia? or to be shot to death with pearls?
215 I know death hath ten thousand several doors
For men to take their exits; and 'tis found
They go on such strange geometrical hinges,
You may open them both ways: any way, for heaven-sake,
So I were out of your whispering. Tell my brothers
220 That I perceive death, now I am well awake,
Best gift is they can give or I can take.
I would fain put off my last woman's-fault,
I 'd not be tedious to you.
 FIRST EXECUT. We are ready.
 DUCH: Dispose my breath how please you; but my body
Bestow upon my women, will you?
225 FIRST EXECUT. Yes.
 DUCH: Pull, and pull strongly, for your able strength
Must pull down heaven upon me:—
Yet stay; heaven-gates are not so highly arch'd
As princes' palaces; they that enter there
230 Must go upon their knees [Kneels].—Come, violent death,
Serve for mandragora to make me sleep!—
Go tell my brothers, when I am laid out,
They then may feed in quiet. [*They strangle her.*]
 BOS: Where 's the waiting-woman?

SCENE TWO                    MODERN

DUCHESS: I forgive them: they're only doing the same as natural diseases.

BOSOLA: Doesn't death frighten you?
DUCHESS: Why would I be afraid of it when I know I'm going to meet my husband and son in heaven?

BOSOLA: But I still think the manner of your death should frighten you. Strangling is a shameful way to die. This rope you're going to be strangled with should terrify you.

DUCHESS: Not a bit: why would the shameful manner of my death frighten me? How would it be better to have my throat cut with diamonds? Or to be smothered with pleasant spices? Or to be shot to death with pearls? I know there are thousands of different ways to die, and the doors to the afterlife have such strange hinges that you may open them both ways [i.e. by pulling or pushing – suicide or murder]. I'd be glad to go through them any way if it means I am away from your scheming. Tell my brothers that I think of death, now I am fully myself, the best gift they could give me. I don't want to be guilty of the woman's fault of talking too much and seeming tedious to you, so I'll be quiet.

FIRST EXECUTIONER: We are ready.

DUCHESS: Do what you want with my breath, but give my body to my women servants, will you?

FIRST EXECUTIONER: Yes.
DUCHESS: Pull strongly on your rope, for your job is to pull heaven down to me. But wait – the gates to heaven aren't the elegant, highly arched ones of princes' palaces – those that enter heaven must do so with humility. [*Kneels*] – Come, violent death, serve as a sedative to make me sleep peacefully! – Go and tell my brothers, when I am dead, they may feed on me undisturbed. [*They strangle her*].

BOSOLA: Where's her maid?

173

Fetch her: some other strangle the children.
[*Enter* CARIOLA]
235 Look you, there sleeps your mistress.
 CARI:     O, you are damn'd
Perpetually for this! My turn is next;
Is 't not so ordered?
 BOS:     Yes, and I am glad
You are so well prepar'd for 't.
 CARI:     You are deceiv'd, sir,
I am not prepar'd for 't, I will not die;
240 I will first come to my answer, and know
How I have offended.
 BOS:     Come despatch her.—
You kept her counsel; now you shall keep ours.
 CARI: I will not die, I must not; I am contracted
To a young gentleman.
 FIRST EXECUT.     Here 's your wedding-ring.

245 CARI: Let me but speak with the duke. I 'll discover
Treason to his person.
 BOS:     Delays:—throttle her.
 FIRST EXECUT. She bites and scratches.
 CARI:     If you kill me now,
I am damn'd; I have not been at confession
This two years.
 BOS: [*To* EXECUTIONERS.] When?
 CARI:     I am quick with child.
 BOS:     Why, then,
250 Your credit 's saved. [*Executioners strangle* CARIOLA.]
     Bear her into the next room;
Let this lie still. [Exeunt the Executioners with the body of CARIOLA.]

SCENE TWO                    MODERN

Fetch her. Someone strangle the children.
    [*Enter* CARIOLA]
Look — there sleeps your mistress.
CARIOLA: Oh, you'll be eternally punished in hell for this! Is it planned for me to be killed next?

BOSOLA: Yes, and I am glad you are so well prepared for it.

CARIOLA: You're wrong. I am not prepared and I will not die. I first want to know what I've done so wrong to deserve death.

BOSOLA: [*To* EXECUTIONERS] Kill her. [*To* CARIOLA] You kept the Duchess's secrets, now you'll keep ours.
CARIOLA: I will not die, I must not. I am engaged to be married to a young gentleman.

FIRST EXECUTIONER: [Showing her the loop of the strangling-rope] Here's your wedding ring.
CARIOLA: Let me speak with Ferdinand. I'll reveal a treasonous plot against him.
BOSOLA: She's stalling. Strangle her.
FIRST EXECUTIONER: Ouch — she's biting and scratching me.
CARIOLA: I'll be damned to hell if you kill me now because I haven't been to confession for two years.

BOSOLA: [*To* EXECUTIONERS] Get on with it.

CARIOLA: You can't kill me — I'm pregnant.
BOSOLA: Then your reputation will be saved if you die before giving birth to an illegitimate child. [EXECUTIONERS *strangle* CARIOLA]. Carry her into the next room; leave the Duchess's body here. [*Exeunt the Executioners with the body of* CARIOLA.]

ORIGINAL            ACT FOUR

### WHAT'S GOING ON?

*The Duchess meets her death with dignity and without fear for two reasons: she believes she'll meet Antonio and her son in heaven, and she sees death as an escape from the hellish, corrupt world around her. The death of such a main character in the fourth act comes as quite a structural shock — normally they die in the final act — and this helps permeate the sense that something unjust has been done, something that goes against the natural*

[*Enter* FERDINAND]

FERD: Is she dead?
BOS: She is what
You'd have her. But here begin your pity: [Shows the Children strangled].
Alas, how have these offended?
FERD: The death
Of young wolves is never to be pitied.
BOS: Fix your eye here.
FERD: Constantly.
255  BOS: Do you not weep?
Other sins only speak; murder shrieks out.
The element of water moistens the earth,
But blood flies upwards and bedews the heavens.
FERD: Cover her face; mine eyes dazzle: she died young.
260  BOS: I think not so; her infelicity
Seem'd to have years too many.
FERD: She and I were twins;
And should I die this instant, I had liv'd
Her time to a minute.
BOS: It seems she was born first:
You have bloodily approv'd the ancient truth,
265  That kindred commonly do worse agree
Than remote strangers.

SCENE TWO　　　　　　MODERN

*order of things.*

*Cariola's death contrasts the Duchess's — Cariola kicks and bites, coming up with any lie she can think of to save her life. While her resistance is admirable, it also highlights the integrity and nobility of the Duchess.*

*Bosola's moral awakening takes a bit of a dip here. His ruthless way of carrying out his task — particularly shocking when he nonchalantly orders the Duchess's children to be strangled — make it harder to see him as someone who's started placing moral values above material reward.*

[*Enter* FERDINAND]

FERDINAND: Is she dead?

BOSOLA: She is, as you wanted. But you should feel pity about this: [Shows the Children strangled]. What did they do wrong?

FERDINAND: The death of animals is never to be pitied.

BOSOLA: Look at them.

FERDINAND: Without flinching.

BOSOLA: Doesn't the sight of them make you weep? Murder is the most appalling sin. Murder is an offence against the heavens.

FERDINAND: Cover up her face, the light of it dazzles my eyes. She died young.

BOSOLA: I don't think so. She had too many years of unhappiness.

FERDINAND: She and I were twins, and if I died right now, I would have lived the same amount of time as her.

BOSOLA: It seems she was born first, as she's the stronger. You have violently proved the ancient truth that relatives have worse conflicts than complete strangers.

FERD: Let me see her face
Again. Why didst thou not pity her? What
An excellent honest man mightst thou have been,
If thou hadst borne her to some sanctuary!
270 Or, bold in a good cause, oppos'd thyself,
With thy advanced sword above thy head,
Between her innocence and my revenge!
I bade thee, when I was distracted of my wits,
Go kill my dearest friend, and thou hast done 't.
275 For let me but examine well the cause:
What was the meanness of her match to me?
Only I must confess I had a hope,
Had she continu'd widow, to have gain'd
An infinite mass of treasure by her death:
280 And that was the main cause,—her marriage,
That drew a stream of gall quite through my heart.
For thee, as we observe in tragedies
That a good actor many times is curs'd
For playing a villain's part, I hate thee for 't,
285 And, for my sake, say, thou hast done much ill well.
 BOS: Let me quicken your memory, for I perceive
You are falling into ingratitude: I challenge
The reward due to my service.
 FERD: I 'll tell thee
What I 'll give thee.
 BOS: Do.
 FERD: I 'll give thee a pardon
For this murder.
 BOS: Ha!
290 FERD: Yes, and 'tis
The largest bounty I can study to do thee.
By what authority didst thou execute
This bloody sentence?
 BOS: By yours.

 FERD: Mine! was I her judge?

SCENE TWO　　　　　　　　MODERN

FERDINAND: Let me see her face again. Why didn't you show her pity? You would have been an excellent, honest man if you had taken her away from here to a safe place! Or shown some boldness in a good cause and defended her innocence from my revenge with a sword in your hands! I asked you to kill my dearest friend when I was out of my mind, and you went and did it.

Let me remind myself of the cause – her marriage to a mean, low-status man. What did that really matter to me? Only that I hoped to inherit lots of wealth when she died, had she remained unmarried. And that was the cause of it all – her marriage, which poisoned my heart.

For you, Bosola, just as a good actor is hated by the audience for performing a villain's part, I hate you for what you've performed, and I say you've done an excellent job of doing me much ill.

BOSOLA: Let me refresh your memory, for I feel you're sounding ungrateful – I've carried out the service you requested and I want my reward.
FERDINAND: I'll tell you what reward I'll give you.

BOSOLA: Do.
FERDINAND: I'll give you a pardon for this murder.

BOSOLA: Ha!

FERDINAND: Yes, and it is the greatest reward I can give you. By whose orders did you carry out this violent punishment?

BOSOLA: By yours.

FERDINAND: Mine?! I was not her judge; it was not for me to decide her punishment.

Did any ceremonial form of law
Doom her to not-being? Did a complete jury
Deliver her conviction up i' the court?
Where shalt thou find this judgment register'd,
Unless in hell? See, like a bloody fool,
Thou'st forfeited thy life, and thou shalt die for 't.

BOS: The office of justice is perverted quite
When one thief hangs another. Who shall dare
To reveal this?

FERD: O, I 'll tell thee;
The wolf shall find her grave, and scrape it up,
Not to devour the corpse, but to discover
The horrid murder.

BOS: You, not I, shall quake for 't.

FERD: Leave me.

BOS: I will first receive my pension.

FERD: You are a villain.

BOS: When your ingratitude
Is judge, I am so.

FERD: O horror,
That not the fear of him which binds the devils
Can prescribe man obedience!—
Never look upon me more.

BOS: Why, fare thee well.
Your brother and yourself are worthy men!
You have a pair of hearts are hollow graves,
Rotten, and rotting others; and your vengeance,
Like two chain'd-bullets, still goes arm in arm:
You may be brothers; for treason, like the plague,
Doth take much in a blood. I stand like one
That long hath ta'en a sweet and golden dream:
I am angry with myself, now that I wake.

FERD: Get thee into some unknown part o' the world,
That I may never see thee.

BOS: Let me know
Wherefore I should be thus neglected. Sir,
I serv'd your tyranny, and rather strove

SCENE TWO          MODERN

No proper process of law decided it was right for her to die. No jury debated and announced her guilt to a court. Where would this judgement against her ever be considered official, except in hell? See, like a bloodthirsty fool, you've given up your life as a penalty for your crime. You will die for it.

BOSOLA: Justice is completely corrupted when one criminal decides the guilt of another. Who would dare to reveal the truth about her murder?

FERDINAND: Oh, I'll tell you: it's inevitable that the truth will come out. A natural, instinctive urge, like a wolf, will uncover her body, not to eat it, but to unveil the truth of what happened.
BOSOLA: It'll be you, not me, who'll be in trouble for it.
FERDINAND: Go away.
BOSOLA: Not before I've got my payment.
FERDINAND: You are a villain.
BOSOLA: When something as villainous as your ingratitude is the judge, then I am a villain.

FERDINAND: Oh horror, that the fear of God is not enough to make man obedient. Never look at me again.


BOSOLA: Well then, fare you well. Your brother and you are fine men indeed! You have a pair of hearts like hollow graves, corrupt, and corrupting others. And your desire for revenge goes arm in arm like two cannonballs chained together to cause greater destruction. You are surely brothers, because treason runs in the blood of families and you're both treasonous. I am like someone who's been bewitched by a dream, and is now angry with himself because he's woken up and been confronted by reality.

FERDINAND: Go to some distant part of the world where I will never see you.
BOSOLA: Tell me why I should be so unfairly treated as this. I carried out your tyrannous orders, and did my best

To satisfy yourself than all the world:
325 And though I loath'd the evil, yet I lov'd
You that did counsel it; and rather sought
To appear a true servant than an honest man.
  FERD: I 'll go hunt the badger by owl-light:
'Tis a deed of darkness. [*Exit.*]
330   BOS: He 's much distracted. Off, my painted honour!
While with vain hopes our faculties we tire,
We seem to sweat in ice and freeze in fire.
What would I do, were this to do again?
I would not change my peace of conscience
335 For all the wealth of Europe.—She stirs; here 's life:—
Return, fair soul, from darkness, and lead mine
Out of this sensible hell:—she 's warm, she breathes:—
Upon thy pale lips I will melt my heart,
To store them with fresh colour.—Who 's there?
340 Some cordial drink!—Alas! I dare not call:
So pity would destroy pity.—Her eye opes,
And heaven in it seems to ope, that late was shut,
To take me up to mercy.
  DUCH: Antonio!
  BOS:     Yes, madam, he is living;
345 The dead bodies you saw were but feign'd statues.
He 's reconcil'd to your brothers; the Pope hath wrought
The atonement.
  DUCH:    Mercy! [*Dies.*]
  BOS: O, she 's gone again! there the cords of life broke.
O sacred innocence, that sweetly sleeps
350 On turtles' feathers, whilst a guilty conscience
Is a black register wherein is writ
All our good deeds and bad, a perspective
That shows us hell! That we cannot be suffer'd
To do good when we have a mind to it!
355 This is manly sorrow;
These tears, I am very certain, never grew
In my mother's milk. My estate is sunk
Below the degree of fear: where were

to do right by you rather than what was right for the world, and though I hated doing evil things, I loved that you instructed them, and wanted more to be a loyal servant to you than to be a good, honest man.

FERDINAND: I'll go and hunt badgers in the night; it is a deed befitting my own darkness.[Exit.]

BOSOLA: He's out of his mind. Ah, I cast off my false honours! My pursuit of status and wealth! We exhaust ourselves by chasing things that can never be achieved; it feels like we're sweating in ice and freezing in fire. What would I change if all this were to happen again? I wouldn't sacrifice my moral integrity, not for all the wealth of Europe. The Duchess! She's moving! She's alive – come back, fair soul, from darkness, and lead my soul out of this physical hell. She's warm to the touch – she's breathing. I will give all my heart to your lips, to bring their colour back. Is anyone there? Bring water! Ah no, I dare not call out, because if Ferdinand hears he'll come back to kill her and my pity for her would have destroyed her. Her eye opens, and it's as if heaven is opening, after long being closed, to offer me mercy.

DUCHESS: Antonio!

BOSOLA: Yes, madam, he's still alive. The dead bodies you saw were just fake statues. The conflict between him and your brothers is resolved, and the Pope has made their agreement official.

DUCHESS: Mercy!       [Dies.]

BOSOLA: Oh, she's gone again! The cords holding her to life are cut. Oh her sacred innocence sleeps on the feathers of turtle doves, while my guilty conscience is a record book detailing all good and bad deeds, and the good ones highlight how evil the bad ones are! It is a shame that we can't be allowed to do good things even when we have a mind to be good!

This is a manly sort of sadness I'm feeling, not the effeminate sort that comes through mothers' milk – it is not a sadness of fear; my situation has sunk to a lower place than fear. Where were

These penitent fountains while she was living?
360 O, they were frozen up! Here is a sight
As direful to my soul as is the sword
Unto a wretch hath slain his father.
Come, I 'll bear thee hence,
And execute thy last will: that 's deliver
365 Thy body to the reverend dispose
Of some good women: that the cruel tyrant
Shall not deny me. Then I 'll post to Milan,
Where somewhat I will speedily enact
Worth my dejection. [*Exit with the body.*]

### WHAT'S GOING ON?
*The sight of his sister's dead body is quite the wake-up call for Ferdinand, who immediately puts the blame on Bosola. Ferdinand's condition from now on will be a torturous one, torn between the sharp, clear insight about what he's done and the animalistic madness this understanding affects him with.*

SCENE TWO          MODERN

these tears of guilt when she was still alive? They were frozen up, and it's too late for them now! Seeing the dead Duchess is as terrible for my soul as it is for the soul of a little boy looking at the sword that has killed his father. Come, I'll carry your body away from here, and carry out your last request by respectfully delivering you to your women. The cruel tyrant Ferdinand can't stop me doing that. Then I'll rush off to Milan, where I'll quickly do something befitting of my depressed state of mind. [*Exit with the body.*]

---

*Bosola seems to finally surrender his pursuit of reward, exploding with an ecstasy of guilt and sadness. But how much do we trust his moral transformation? Are his words to the Duchess, when she pops back into life, kind or cruel? Will his vague plans to do "something" in Milan be motivated by a moral revenge for the Duchess, or a materialistic revenge for being denied his reward?*

ACT FIVE

Scene One

[*Enter* ANTONIO *and* DELIO]

ANT: What think you of my hope of reconcilement
To the Arragonian brethren?
DELIO.   I misdoubt it;
For though they have sent their letters of safe-conduct
For your repair to Milan, they appear
5   But nets to entrap you. The Marquis of Pescara,
Under whom you hold certain land in cheat,
Much 'gainst his noble nature hath been mov'd
To seize those lands; and some of his dependants
Are at this instant making it their suit
10 To be invested in your revenues.
I cannot think they mean well to your life
That do deprive you of your means of life,
Your living.
ANT:   You are still an heretic
To any safety I can shape myself.
15   DELIO. Here comes the marquis: I will make myself
Petitioner for some part of your land,
To know whither it is flying.
ANT:   I pray, do. [*Withdraws*.]
  [*Enter* PESCARA]
DELIO. Sir, I have a suit to you.
PES.   To me?
DELIO.   An easy one:
There is the Citadel of Saint Bennet,
20 With some demesnes, of late in the possession
Of Antonio Bologna,—please you bestow them on me.

SCENE ONE          MODERN

*[Enter ANTONIO and DELIO — in a public place in Milan]*

ANTONIO: What do you think my chances are of making peace with Ferdinand and the Cardinal?

DELIO: Not great. Although they sent guarantees of your safety for your journey here to Milan, I think these were just to lure you into a trap, concealing bad intentions with kindness. Because of your banishment, the Marquis of Pescara has decided, against his good and noble nature, to reclaim the land you own in cheat (which means the lord can lawfully reclaim property if the owner dies or commits a crime). Some of Pescara's people are currently showing a keen interest in taking over your wealth and property. I do not think these people who seek to deprive you of your way of living can have any good intentions towards your life.

ANTONIO: You still disbelieve in my ability to keep myself safe.
DELIO: Here comes the marquis. I will ask him for some of your land, just so we can find out who it's being given away to.

ANTONIO: Please, do.   [*Withdraws.*]
       [*Enter* PESCARA]

DELIO: Sir, I have some business with you.
PESCARA: With me?
DELIO: A simple affair: the Citadel of Saint Bennet, with some land attached, was until recently in the possession of Antonio Bologna. I ask that you please give it to me.

PES. You are my friend; but this is such a suit,
Nor fit for me to give, nor you to take.
DELIO. No, sir?
PES. I will give you ample reason for 't
25 Soon in private:—here 's the cardinal's mistress.
    [*Enter* JULIA]
JULIA: My lord, I am grown your poor petitioner,
And should be an ill beggar, had I not
A great man's letter here, the cardinal's,
To court you in my favour.    [*Gives a letter.*]
PES.    He entreats for you
30 The Citadel of Saint Bennet, that belong'd
To the banish'd Bologna.
JULIA:    Yes.
PES. I could not have thought of a friend I could rather
Pleasure with it: 'tis yours.
JULIA:    Sir, I thank you;
And he shall know how doubly I am engag'd
35 Both in your gift, and speediness of giving
Which makes your grant the greater.    [*Exit.*]
ANT:    How they fortify
Themselves with my ruin!
DELIO.    Sir, I am
Little bound to you.
PES.    Why?
DELIO. Because you deni'd this suit to me, and gave 't
To such a creature.
40 PES.    Do you know what it was?
It was Antonio's land; not forfeited
By course of law, but ravish'd from his throat
By the cardinal's entreaty. It were not fit
I should bestow so main a piece of wrong
45 Upon my friend; 'tis a gratification
Only due to a strumpet, for it is injustice.
Shall I sprinkle the pure blood of innocents
To make those followers I call my friends
Look ruddier upon me? I am glad

SCENE ONE　　　　　　　MODERN

PESCARA: You are my friend, but it's not right for me to give this to you, nor right for you to take it.

DELIO: Why not, sir?

PESCARA: I will explain to you in private – here's the Cardinal's mistress.

　　　[*Enter* JULIA]

JULIA: My lord, I come here to humbly ask you for something, and would just be a lowly beggar if I didn't have this letter from the Cardinal which asks you to show me your favour.　　[*Gives a letter.*]

PESCARA: He asks me to give you the Citadel of Saint Bennet, that belonged to the banished Antonio.

JULIA: Yes.

PESCARA: I couldn't think of anyone else I'd rather give it to. It's yours.

JULIA: Sir, I thank you, and I'll tell the Cardinal how I am doubly grateful to you – for your gift, and for the speed with which it was given, which makes your gift even greater.
　　　　　　　　　　　　　　　　　　　　　　　　[*Exit.*]

ANTONIO: [*Aside*] How they exploit my ruin for their own advantage!

DELIO: Sir, I feel our friendship is a little wounded.

PESCARA: Why?

DELIO: Because you refused to give Antonio's property to me, and gave it instead to that creature.

PESCARA: Do you know what it was? That was Antonio's land, not taken from him lawfully, but ripped away from him by the Cardinal's wishes. It wouldn't be right for me to give something so wrongfully obtained to my friend; it is a gift only appropriate for a whore, because it is stained by injustice.

Should I make gifts of the things that cause innocent people suffering, just to make people I call friends look more fondly

50 This land, ta'en from the owner by such wrong,
Returns again unto so foul an use
As salary for his lust. Learn, good Delio,
To ask noble things of me, and you shall find
I 'll be a noble giver.
   DELIO.     You instruct me well.
55 ANT: Why, here 's a man now would fright impudence
From sauciest beggars.
   PES.     Prince Ferdinand 's come to Milan,
Sick, as they give out, of an apoplexy;
But some say 'tis a frenzy: I am going
To visit him. [*Exit.*]
   ANT:     'Tis a noble old fellow.
60 DELIO. What course do you mean to take, Antonio?
   ANT: This night I mean to venture all my fortune,
Which is no more than a poor ling'ring life,
To the cardinal's worst of malice. I have got
Private access to his chamber; and intend
65 To visit him about the mid of night,
As once his brother did our noble duchess.
It may be that the sudden apprehension
Of danger,—for I 'll go in mine own shape,—
When he shall see it fraight with love and duty,
70 May draw the poison out of him, and work
A friendly reconcilement. If it fail,
Yet it shall rid me of this infamous calling;
For better fall once than be ever falling.
   DELIO. I 'll second you in all danger; and howe'er,
75 My life keeps rank with yours.
   ANT: You are still my lov'd and best friend. [*Exeunt.*]

upon me? I am glad that this land, so immorally taken from its owner, goes to such immoral purpose as being the Cardinal's payment to his prostitute, Julia. Learn, good Delio, to ask for noble, moral things from me and you will find I'll give them generously.

DELIO: You teach me well.

ANTONIO: [*Aside*] Gosh – this is a man who could frighten rudeness out of the lowliest scoundrels.

PESCARA: Prince Ferdinand has come to Milan, sick, people say, with a brain haemorrhage, but there's also a rumour he's gone mad. I'm going to visit him.   [*Exit.*]

ANTONIO: What a noble fellow.
DELIO: What's your plan now, Antonio?
ANTONIO: Tonight I'm going to gamble everything, which for me now is nothing more than my life, on the Cardinal's ill feelings toward me. I have (somehow) managed to arrange access to his private chamber, and I'm going to visit him at midnight, as Ferdinand once visited our noble Duchess.

I'm hoping that when he sees my fear of him, and how it is so full of love and duty, all the poison of his bad feelings for me will be drawn out of him, and we'll be able to make peace in a friendly way. If this fails, at least it will be the end of everything. It's better to fall once (by dying) than to spend your whole life constantly falling.

DELIO: I'll back you up. Whatever happens, I'll be with you.

ANTONIO: You are still my loved, and best, friend.
[*Exeunt.*]

ORIGINAL                    ACT FIVE

## WHAT'S GOING ON?
*After the previous scene, Antonio's desire to make friends with the Cardinal and Ferdinand seem a bit…pathetic – but of course he doesn't know what's happened to his wife. Antonio's inefficacy and passiveness is further highlighted when he has to quietly watch while his property is carved up and handed out to other people.*

Scene Two

[*Enter* PESCARA *and* DOCTOR]

    PES.  Now, doctor, may I visit your patient?
    DOC.  If 't please your lordship; but he 's instantly
To take the air here in the gallery
By my direction.
    PES.      Pray thee, what 's his disease?

5    DOC.  A very pestilent disease, my lord,
They call lycanthropia.
    PES.      What 's that?
I need a dictionary to 't.
    DOC.      I 'll tell you.
In those that are possess'd with 't there o'erflows
Such melancholy humour they imagine
10    Themselves to be transformed into wolves;
Steal forth to church-yards in the dead of night,
And dig dead bodies up: as two nights since
One met the duke 'bout midnight in a lane
Behind Saint Mark's church, with the leg of a man
15    Upon his shoulder; and he howl'd fearfully;
Said he was a wolf, only the difference

SCENE TWO        MODERN

*Pescara's reasons for refusing to give Antonio's land to Delio is an important part of the play's critique against materialism, making the argument that value is not only determined so much by the material property of something as its moral associations.*

*Antonio resolves to go to the Cardinal and make up with him, even if it costs him his life, and good old Delio promises his faithful support.*

[*Enter* PESCARA *and* DOCTOR — *in the residence of the* CARDINAL *and* FERDINAND]

PESCARA: Now, doctor, may I visit your patient, the Lord Ferdinand?
DOCTOR: If you want, but I've ordered him to come out of his room for some fresh air.
PESCARA: Please tell me, what disease is her suffering from?
DOCTOR: A vicious one, my lord, which they call lycanthropia.
PESCARA: What's that? I need to look it up in a dictionary.

DOCTOR: I can tell you. People struck with lycanthropia suffer such an imbalance of the four humours, with an overflowing excess of the black humour melancholia, that they believe they are transformed into werewolves. They even sneak into churchyards in the middle of the night and dig up dead bodies. Just two nights ago someone met Ferdinand in a lane behind St. Mark's church carrying the leg of a dead man on his shoulder. Apparently, Ferdinand howled fearfully and said he was a wolf, explaining the only difference for him

Was, a wolf's skin was hairy on the outside,
His on the inside; bade them take their swords,
Rip up his flesh, and try. Straight I was sent for,
And, having minister'd to him, found his grace
Very well recover'd.

PES. I am glad on 't.

DOC. Yet not without some fear
Of a relapse. If he grow to his fit again,
I 'll go a nearer way to work with him
Than ever Paracelsus dream'd of; if
They 'll give me leave, I 'll buffet his madness out of him.
Stand aside; he comes.

[*Enter* FERDINAND, CARDINAL, MALATESTI, *and* BOSOLA]

FERD: Leave me.

MAL. Why doth your lordship love this solitariness?

FERD: Eagles commonly fly alone: they are crows, daws, and starlings that flock together. Look, what 's that follows me?

MAL. Nothing, my lord.

FERD: Yes.

MAL. 'Tis your shadow.

FERD: Stay it; let it not haunt me.

MAL. Impossible, if you move, and the sun shine.

FERD: I will throttle it. [Throws himself down on his shadow.]

MAL. O, my lord, you are angry with nothing.

FERD: You are a fool: how is 't possible I should catch my shadow, unless I fall upon 't? When I go to hell, I mean to carry a bribe; for, look you, good gifts evermore make way for the worst persons.

PES. Rise, good my lord.

FERD: I am studying the art of patience.

PES. 'Tis a noble virtue.

FERD: To drive six snails before me from this town to Moscow; neither use goad nor whip to them, but let

SCENE TWO   MODERN

was a wolf's skin is hairy on the outside, whereas Ferdinand's is hairy on the inside. He suggested they cut him open with their swords so they could see for themselves. Immediately I was summoned, and, after I tended to him, Ferdinand was well recovered.

PESCARA: I'm glad to hear it.

DOCTOR: But it's still possible he could get worse. If he sinks into his delirium again, I'll give him an even more extreme treatment than those of the German doctor Paracelsus, who was known for his extreme practices. If I'm given permission, I will use brute force to knock the madness out of him. Stand back — here he comes.

[*Enter* FERDINAND, CARDINAL, MALATESTI, *and* BOSOLA]

FERDINAND: Leave me alone.

MALATESTI: Why do you always want to be by yourself?

FERDINAND: It's natural for the eagle to fly alone. Only the lowly crows, daws and starlings fly in groups. Look — what's that following me?

MALATESTI: There's nothing, my lord.

FERDINAND: There is.

MALATESTI: It's just your shadow.

FERDINAND: Make it stop; stop it from haunting me.

MALATESTI: That's impossible, unless you stop moving, or the sun stops shining.

FERDINAND: I will strangle it! [*Throws himself down on his shadow.*]

MALATESTI: Oh, my lord, you're fighting with nothing!

FERDINAND: You are a fool. How else can I catch my shadow, unless I fall on it? When I go to hell, I will take bribes, because offering good gifts make always make up for being a terrible person.

PESCARA: Stand up, my good lord.

FERDINAND: I am learning how to be patient.

PESCARA: It's a noble thing, to be patient.

FERDINAND: I plan to follow behind six snails from here to Moscow, without encouraging them on or whipping them, but

them take their own time;—the patient'st man i' th'
world match me for an experiment:—an I 'll crawl after
like a sheep-biter.

CARD: Force him up. [*They raise him.*]

FERD: Use me well, you were best. What I have done,
I have done: I 'll confess nothing.

DOC. Now let me come to him.—Are you mad, my
lord? are you out of your princely wits?

FERD:    What 's he?

PES.    Your doctor.

FERD: Let me have his beard saw'd off, and his eyebrows fil'd more civil.

DOC. I must do mad tricks with him, for that 's the
only way on 't.—I have brought your grace a
salamander's skin to keep you from sun-burning.

FERD: I have cruel sore eyes.

DOC. The white of a cockatrix's egg is present
remedy.

FERD: Let it be a new-laid one, you were best.
Hide me from him: physicians are like kings,—
They brook no contradiction.

DOC. Now he begins to fear me: now let me alone
with him.

CARD: How now! put off your gown!

DOC. Let me have some forty urinals filled with
rosewater: he and I 'll go pelt one another with them.—
Now he begins to fear me.—Can you fetch a frisk, sir?—
Let him go, let him go, upon my peril: I find by his eye
he stands in awe of me; I 'll make him as tame as a
dormouse.

FERD: Can you fetch your frisks, sir!

letting them go at their own pace. I'll go with the world's most patient man to measure my own patience against his. And I'll crawl behind like a sheepdog.
CARDINAL: Force him up.  [*They raise him.*]
FERDINAND: You'd be wise to treat me well. I have done what I have done, but I won't confess it.

DOCTOR: Now let me near him. – Are you mad, my lord? Are you out of your princely mind?
FERDINAND: Who's he?
PESCARA: Your doctor.

FERDINAND: Let me have his beard sawed off, and his eyebrows filed to look more refined.
DOCTOR: It's a common, if controversial, practice to treat madness with madness, and that's the only way to help him. [*To FERDINAND*] I have brought your grace a salamander's skin, which is said to be fireproof, to protect you from sunburn.
FERDINAND: My cruel eyes are sore from what they've been seeing.
DOCTOR: The white of the egg of a cockatrice [mythical creature] will help with that.
FERDINAND: Make sure it's a fresh egg. [*To others*] Hide me away from him. Doctors are like kings – they don't tolerate anyone disagreeing with them.
DOCTOR: It's working – he's beginning to fear me. Leave me alone with him.

CARDINAL: [*To FERDINAND*] Get ready – you'll need to take off your gown in preparation for more extreme treatments!
DOCTOR: Bring me about forty urinals filled with rose-flavoured water: Ferdinand and I will have a water-fight with them. (Now he begins to fear me.) [*To FERDINAND*] Can you dance a jig, sir? – [*To others*] Let him go, let him go, I swear it's safe – I can tell by the way he looks at me that he's intimidated by me. I'll make him as tame as a dormouse.
FERDINAND: Can you dance your jigs, sir?!

75   —I will stamp him into a cullis, flay off his skin to cover
one of the anatomie this rogue hath set i' th' cold
yonder in Barber-Chirurgeon's-hall.—Hence, hence! you
are all of you like beasts for sacrifice. [Throws the
DOCTOR down and beats him.] There 's nothing left
80   of you but tongue and belly, flattery and lechery. [Exit.]


   PES.  Doctor, he did not fear you thoroughly.

   DOC.  True; I was somewhat too forward.

   BOS:  Mercy upon me, what a fatal judgment
Hath fall'n upon this Ferdinand!
   PES.       Knows your grace
85 What accident hath brought unto the prince
This strange distraction?
   CARD:  [aside] I must feign somewhat.—Thus they say
it grew.
You have heard it rumour'd, for these many years
None of our family dies but there is seen
90 The shape of an old woman, which is given
By tradition to us to have been murder'd
By her nephews for her riches. Such a figure
One night, as the prince sat up late at 's book,
Appear'd to him; when crying out for help,
95 The gentleman of 's chamber found his grace
All on a cold sweat, alter'd much in face
And language: since which apparition,
He hath grown worse and worse, and I much fear
He cannot live.
   BOS:     Sir, I would speak with you.
100   PES.  We 'll leave your grace,
Wishing to the sick prince, our noble lord,
All health of mind and body.
   CARD:     You are most welcome. [Exeunt
PESCARA, MALATESTI, and DOCTOR.]

SCENE TWO          MODERN

[*To others, about the doctor*] I will pound him into a soup; I'll flay off his skin and use it to cover one of the medical skeletons this dodgy doctor has supplied to the cold halls of the anatomical museum at the Barber-Surgeons' Hall. Go away, go away! All of you are like beasts that are slaughtered. [*Throws the* DOCTOR *down and beats him.*] Like those beasts, there's nothing left of you but your deceiving, flattering tongues and your greedy, lustful bellies.

[*Exit.*]

PESCARA: Well, doctor, he didn't seem sufficiently frightened of you.

DOCTOR: True; I was a bit too over-the-top to be convincing.

BOSOLA: [*Aside*] My goodness, what a terrible punishment this is for Ferdinand!

PESCARA: [*To the* CARDINAL] Do you know what's caused Ferdinand's madness?

CARDINAL: [*Aside*] I need to put on an act. [*End aside*] They say it came about like this: you've heard the rumour that for many years every member of our family sees, before dying, the figure of an old woman who, according to tradition, was murdered by her nephews so they could inherit her wealth. It was this ghostly figure of an old lady that Ferdinand saw late one night when he was reading.

When he cried out for help, Ferdinand's attendant found him in a cold sweat, and with a dramatic change in his facial appearance and speech. Since seeing that ghost, Ferdinand has gotten worse and worse, and I worry he won't survive.

BOSOLA: [*To the* CARDINAL] Sir, I'd like to speak with you in private.

PESCARA: We'll leave, with our best wishes for the healthy mind and body of our prince Ferdinand.

CARDINAL: You are most welcome. [*Exeunt* PESCARA, MALATESTI, *and* DOCTOR.]

ORIGINAL                    ACT FIVE

Are you come? so.—[*Aside.*] This fellow must not know
By any means I had intelligence
In our duchess' death; for, though I counsell'd it,
The full of all th' engagement seem'd to grow
From Ferdinand.—Now, sir, how fares our sister?
I do not think but sorrow makes her look
Like to an oft-dy'd garment: she shall now
Take comfort from me. Why do you look so wildly?
O, the fortune of your master here the prince
Dejects you; but be you of happy comfort:
If you 'll do one thing for me I 'll entreat,
Though he had a cold tomb-stone o'er his bones,
I 'd make you what you would be.
BOS:     Any thing;
Give it me in a breath, and let me fly to 't.
They that think long small expedition win,
For musing much o' th' end cannot begin.

---

### WHAT'S GOING ON?
*Ferdinand is suffering from a psychological condition called lycanthropia, in which he believes he is a werewolf. In Webster's time, this wouldn't have been regarded as a psychological condition, but as a consequence of an imbalance among the four humours (bodily fluids), as the doctor explains. James I, the king during Webster's time and known for his interest in witchcraft, believed himself that werewolves were people suffering delusion brought about by this humour imbalance. The audience, however, will be alert to the*

---

[*Enter* JULIA]

JULIA: Sir, will you come into supper?
CARD:     I am busy; leave me.
JULIA [*aside.*] What an excellent shape hath that fellow! [*Exit.*]
CARD: "Tis thus. Antonio lurks here in Milan:
Inquire him out, and kill him. While he lives,

So you're here? [*Aside*] This Bosola must not by any means find out that I had knowledge of the Duchess's death. Although I advised that she be killed, it was Ferdinand who really made her death come about. [*End aside.*] Now, sir, how's our Duchess doing?

I can't help but think her sad mood makes her look like a garment gone pale from being too frequently dyed; it's time I showed her more comfort. Why do you look so angry? Oh, Ferdinand has neglected you, but be comforted. Although Ferdinand was as cold as a tomb-stone toward you, if you do just one thing for me, I'll give you what you want.

BOSOLA: I'll do anything. Tell me immediately, and I'll get straight on it. Those who think too long about doing something never actually get around to doing it and therefore gain nothing.

---

*psychological roots of Ferdinand's madness, and see it as an externalisation of his violent, animalistic desires and impulses. Just as the Duchess was destroyed by her private life being exposed to the public gaze, Ferdinand's dramatic status is destroyed by this exposure of his private internal nature, making him an object of ridicule on the stage.*
*The Cardinal, who we learn here ordered the death of the Duchess, desperately keeps his secrets under wraps.*

*Bosola remains very willing to follow his orders — is this just an act, or does he still have hopes of getting his reward despite his remarks at the end of Act Four?*

---

[*Enter* JULIA]

JULIA: Sir, are you coming to supper?
CARDINAL: I'm busy; leave me.
JULIA: [*Aside — referring to* BOSOLA] What an excellent figure that man has! [*Exit.*]
CARDINAL: The task is this: Antonio is lurking somewhere here in Milan. Seek him out, and kill him. While he's alive,

Our sister cannot marry; and I have thought
Of an excellent match for her. Do this, and style me
Thy advancement.
125   BOS: But by what means shall I find him out?
   CARD: There is a gentleman call'd Delio
Here in the camp, that hath been long approv'd
His loyal friend. Set eye upon that fellow;
Follow him to mass; may be Antonio,
130 Although he do account religion
But a school-name, for fashion of the world
May accompany him; or else go inquire out
Delio's confessor, and see if you can bribe
Him to reveal it. There are a thousand ways
135 A man might find to trace him; as to known
What fellows haunt the Jews for taking up
Great sums of money, for sure he 's in want;
Or else to go to the picture-makers, and learn
Who bought her picture lately: some of these
Happily may take.
140   BOS:      Well, I 'll not freeze i' th' business:
I would see that wretched thing, Antonio,
Above all sights i' th' world.
   CARD:      Do, and be happy. [*Exit.*]
   BOS: This fellow doth breed basilisks in 's eyes,
He 's nothing else but murder; yet he seems
145 Not to have notice of the duchess' death.
'Tis his cunning: I must follow his example;
There cannot be a surer way to trace
Than that of an old fox.
      [*Re-enter* JULIA, *with a pistol*]
   JULIA: So, sir, you are well met.
   BOS:      How Now!
   JULIA: Nay, the doors are fast enough:
150 Now, sir, I will make you confess your treachery.
   BOS: Treachery!
   JULIA:      Yes, confess to me
Which of my women 'twas you hir'd to put

## SCENE TWO — MODERN

the Duchess can't marry, and I've come up with an excellent husband for her. Do this, and tell me what you want in payment.

BOSOLA: But how am I supposed to find him?
CARDINAL: There is a gentleman called Delio in the military camp who's been Antonio's loyal friend for a long time. Find Delio and follow him to mass at church. It may be that Antonio, although he only considers religion a nickname and doesn't take it seriously, will go to mass with him just because it's what other people do. Or, go and find the priest who takes Delio's confession and bribe him to find out Antonio's location.

There are thousands of ways a man can be found. Antonio is surely in need of money, so find out who the fellows are that follow the Jewish money-lenders around. Or go to the picture makers and learn who brought a picture of the Duchess recently (as Antonio will need a substitute for the Duchess herself). Some of these perhaps will work.

BOSOLA: Well, I won't hesitate to get on with it. I would rather see that wretched thing Antonio than anything else in the world.
CARDINAL: Do, and be happy.   [*Exit.*]

BOSOLA: This Cardinal's eyes are those of basilisks, who kill anyone they look at. He is the embodiment of murder, and yet he seems to know nothing about the Duchess's murder. I suspect he's being deceptive, and I must do the same. There's no better example to follow than that of a cunning old fox.

   [*Re-enter JULIA, with a pistol*]
JULIA: I am pleased to see you, sir.
BOSOLA: Oh no!

JULIA: It's no good trying to get away — the doors are locked tight. Now, sir, I will make you admit to your crimes.
BOSOLA: My crimes?!
JULIA: Yes. Confess to me which of my servants you bribed to put

Love-powder into my drink?
 BOS: Love-powder!
 JULIA: Yes, when I was at Malfi.
155 Why should I fall in love with such a face else?
I have already suffer'd for thee so much pain,
The only remedy to do me good
Is to kill my longing.
 BOS: Sure, your pistol holds
Nothing but perfumes or kissing-comfits.
Excellent lady!
160 You have a pretty way on 't to discover
Your longing. Come, come, I 'll disarm you,
And arm you thus: yet this is wondrous strange.
 JULIA: Compare thy form and my eyes together,
You 'll find my love no such great miracle.
165 Now you 'll say
I am wanton: this nice modesty in ladies
Is but a troublesome familiar
That haunts them.
 BOS: Know you me, I am a blunt soldier.

 JULIA: The better:
170 Sure, there wants fire where there are no lively sparks
Of roughness.
 BOS: And I want compliment.
 JULIA: Why, ignorance
In courtship cannot make you do amiss,
If you have a heart to do well.

 BOS: You are very fair.
 JULIA: Nay, if you lay beauty to my charge,
I must plead unguilty.
175 BOS: Your bright eyes
Carry a quiver of darts in them sharper
Than sun-beams.
 JULIA: You will mar me with commendation,
Put yourself to the charge of courting me,
Whereas now I woo you.

SCENE TWO          MODERN

love-powder into my drink.
BOSOLA: Love-powder?!
JULIA: Yes, when I was at Malfi. How else would I fall in love with such a horrific face as yours? I have already suffered so much pain in longing for you; the only cure is to kill the source of my longing (you).

BOSOLA: Surely your pistol is loaded with nothing but perfume or breath-fresheners. Incredible lady! You have an unusual way of expressing your desire for me. Come, come, I'll take your gun away from you (disarm you), and arm you like this [embraces her]. Well, this is all very strange — in a wonderful way.

JULIA: Compare your unattractive shape with my attraction for you and you'll realise my love for you is no miraculous, wonderful thing (it is just a primitive desire; a raw need for intimacy). Now this will make you think I'm lustful: I believe ladies' modesty is like an annoying little spirit that follows them around and stops them pursuing their true desires.
BOSOLA: You know me — I'm not modest; I'm just a blunt soldier.
JULIA: And I like you better for being rough. There's a lack of passion where there's no rough edges to spark up the fire of it.
BOSOLA: I lack the ability to give flattering compliments.
JULIA: It doesn't matter — not knowing what to say in romantic situations won't make you do wrong, so long as your heart is full of good intention. [Or, "do well" could allude to sexual performance.]
BOSOLA: You're very pretty.
JULIA: Oh no, if you accuse me of beauty, I must plead innocence.
BOSOLA: Your bright eyes are full of darts (like Cupid, and predatory) sharper than sunbeams.
JULIA: You will dirty me with false compliments like that. Pull yourself together and put yourself to the task of flirting with me properly, whereas at the moment I'm leading the flirtation.

180   BOS: [*Aside.*] I have it, I will work upon this creature.—
Let us grow most amorously familiar:
If the great cardinal now should see me thus,
Would he not count me a villain?

  JULIA: No; he might count me a wanton,
185 Not lay a scruple of offence on you;
For if I see and steal a diamond,
The fault is not i' th' stone, but in me the thief
That purloins it. I am sudden with you.
We that are great women of pleasure use to cut off
190 These uncertain wishes and unquiet longings,
And in an instant join the sweet delight
And the pretty excuse together. Had you been i' th' street,
Under my chamber-window, even there
I should have courted you.
  BOS: O, you are an excellent lady!
195   JULIA: Bid me do somewhat for you presently
To express I love you.
  BOS:     I will; and if you love me,
Fail not to effect it.
The cardinal is grown wondrous melancholy;
Demand the cause, let him not put you off
200 With feign'd excuse; discover the main ground on 't.
  JULIA: Why would you know this?
  BOS:     I have depended on him,
And I hear that he is fall'n in some disgrace
With the emperor: if he be, like the mice
That forsake falling houses, I would shift
205 To other dependance.
  JULIA:     You shall not need
Follow the wars: I 'll be your maintenance.
  BOS: And I your loyal servant: but I cannot
Leave my calling.

SCENE TWO  MODERN

BOSOLA: [Aside] I know what to do: I'll manipulate this creature [end aside]. Then let's get to know each other more closely, as lovers. Say, if our almighty Cardinal were to see me like this with you, his mistress, wouldn't he think me a villain?

JULIA: No. He might think me lustful, but wouldn't put the slightest bit of blame on you, because if I see a diamond like you, and steal it, the blame is not with the diamond but with me, the thief. I'm being really forward with you. We women who enjoy (sexual) pleasure make it our practice to not bother with sitting quietly longing for someone, instead we just grab what we want, and close the gap between the pretty flirtation and the sweet delight (of sex).

I don't care who sees us — even if you were out in public in the street, I would still want to flirt with you.

BOSOLA: Oh, you're a wonderful lady!

JULIA: Ask me to do something for you, so I can prove my love for you.

BOSOLA: I will, and if you love me, make sure you do it. The Cardinal has become incredibly moody. Find out the reason why, and don't let him trick you with lies. Discover the real reason for it.

JULIA: Why do you care about the Cardinal?

BOSOLA: I rely on him for payment, and I hear that he's fallen into disgrace with the emperor. If that's the case, then like mice that flee from falling houses I will find someone else to rely on.

JULIA: You don't need to be involved in all that conflict. You don't need to rely on anyone but me — I'll take care of you.

BOSOLA: And I will be your loyal servant — however, I cannot leave my calling (of being a spy/assassin/dogsbody for high-status people).

ORIGINAL                                    ACT FIVE

210   JULIA:     Not leave an ungrateful
      General for the love of a sweet lady!
      You are like some cannot sleep in feather-beds,
      But must have blocks for their pillows.
        BOS:     Will you do this?
        JULIA: Cunningly.
        BOS: To-morrow I'll expect th' intelligence.

        JULIA: To-morrow! get you into my cabinet;
215   You shall have it with you. Do not delay me,
      No more than I do you: I am like one
      That is condemn'd; I have my pardon promis'd,
      But I would see it seal'd. Go, get you in:
      You shall see my wind my tongue about his heart
220   Like a skein of silk. [*Exit* BOSOLA.]

---

### WHAT'S GOING ON?
*Julia's taken a shine to Bosola, and to prove her love for him will obey Bosola's request that she discover what secrets the Cardinal is hiding. What with this bizarre flirtation, and Ferdinand howling at his own shadow, Act Five does start to feel pretty deranged — which is surely Webster's purposeful way of showing*

---

        [*Re-enter* CARDINAL]
        CARD:     Where are you?
          [*Enter* Servants]
        SERVANTS.     Here.
        CARD: Let none, upon your lives, have conference
      With the Prince Ferdinand, unless I know it.—
      [Aside] In this distraction he may reveal
      The murder. [*Exeunt* Servants.]
225       Yond's my lingering consumption:
      I am weary of her, and by any means
      Would be quit of.
        JULIA:     How now, my lord! what ails you?

208

SCENE TWO                    MODERN

JULIA: You wouldn't leave someone who shows you no gratitude for the love a sweet lady like me? You are like someone who rejects luxury in favour of the hard life.

BOSOLA: Will you do it?
JULIA: Yes, and I'll do it cleverly.
BOSOLA: Tomorrow I'll be expecting you to tell me what you've found out.
JULIA: Tomorrow?! Get into my cupboard and you'll know it in an instant. Don't faff about with me, just as I don't with you. I am like someone who's been sentenced to execution — I've been verbally promised a pardon, but I want to see it written officially [i.e. if by doing what you've asked I can prove I love you, then it will make our love more official/real — so I'm keen to get on with it]. Go on, get in. You will see me manipulate him with all the smoothness of a strip of silk.                    [Exit BOSOLA.]

---

*the impact of the Duchess's death. All this is the sort of chaos and disarray that comes with the absence of a moral, measured hand at the helm.*

*Julia's mode of love contrasts and highlights the Duchess's. Julia's love is a raw need demanding urgent satisfaction, and situates Bosola as a physical body that can satisfy it, whereas the Duchess loved Antonio for his value as a human being.*

---

[Re-enter the CARDINAL]
CARDINAL: Where are you?
    [Enter Servants]
SERVANTS: Here.
CARDINAL: Swear on your lives none of you will speak with Ferdinand unless I know about it. [Aside] As he's going mad, he might accidentally reveal the truth about the murder of the Duchess. [Exeunt Servants.]

There is my disease that won't leave me alone [he's seen Julia] — I am sick of her, and would by any means be free from her.
JULIA: Oh hello, my lord! What's the matter?

CARD: Nothing,
JULIA: O, you are much alter'd:
Come, I must be your secretary, and remove
This lead from off your bosom: what 's the matter?
CARD: I may not tell you.
JULIA: Are you so far in love with sorrow
You cannot part with part of it? Or think you
I cannot love your grace when you are sad
As well as merry? Or do you suspect
I, that have been a secret to your heart
These many winters, cannot be the same
Unto your tongue?
CARD: Satisfy thy longing,—
The only way to make thee keep my counsel
Is, not to tell thee.
JULIA: Tell your echo this,
Or flatterers, that like echoes still report
What they hear though most imperfect, and not me;
For if that you be true unto yourself,
I 'll know.
CARD: Will you rack me?
JULIA: No, judgment shall
Draw it from you: it is an equal fault,
To tell one's secrets unto all or none.
CARD: The first argues folly.
JULIA: But the last tyranny.

CARD: Very well: why, imagine I have committed
Some secret deed which I desire the world
May never hear of.
JULIA: Therefore may not I know it?
You have conceal'd for me as great a sin
As adultery. Sir, never was occasion
For perfect trial of my constancy
Till now: sir, I beseech you—
CARD: You 'll repent it.
JULIA: Never.

SCENE TWO                    MODERN

CARDINAL: Nothing.
JULIA: Oh, you're not your normal self. Come, I must be your assistant, and help you remove this weight of gloom from your chest. What's the matter?
CARDINAL: I cannot tell you.
JULIA: Are you so obsessed with your sadness that you can't be separated from it? Or do you worry I won't love you as much when you're sad as when you're happy? Or do you suspect that I, who have been faithful to your love these many years, can't keep a secret of the words you say to me?

CARDINAL: Get over your desire to know. The only way I can know you'll keep my secrets is not to tell them to you.

JULIA: Tell that to your echo. Or to your flatterers. It's flatterers and echoes that need to be told not to repeat what they hear, not me. By telling your secret to me you'll only be telling yourself, as I am your other self.

CARDINAL: Are you going to torture a confession out of me?
JULIA: No. God will draw it from you when He judges you. Therefore it ultimately makes no difference whether you tell your secrets to everyone or to no one.

CARDINAL: Telling them to everyone is foolishness.
JULIA: But telling them to no one is what a tyrant does, as he's trying to hide how his rule is unjust.
CARDINAL: Okay then. Imagine I have committed a secret act which I want no one in the world to ever hear of.

JULIA: Then why shouldn't I know of it? You have kept my adultery secret from the word. This is the perfect opportunity to prove my trustworthiness. Please, I beg you —


CARDINAL: You'll regret it.
JULIA: Never.

211

CARD: It hurries thee to ruin: I'll not tell thee.
Be well advis'd, and think what danger 'tis
To receive a prince's secrets. They that do,
Had need have their breasts hoop'd with adamant
To contain them. I pray thee, yet be satisfi'd;
Examine thine own frailty; 'tis more easy
To tie knots than unloose them. 'Tis a secret
That, like a ling'ring poison, may chance lie
Spread in thy veins, and kill thee seven year hence.

JULIA: Now you dally with me.
CARD: No more; thou shalt know it.
By my appointment the great Duchess of Malfi
And two of her young children, four nights since,
Were strangl'd.
JULIA: O heaven! sir, what have you done!
CARD: How now? How settles this? Think you your bosom
Will be a grave dark and obscure enough
For such a secret?
JULIA: You have undone yourself, sir.
CARD: Why?
JULIA: It lies not in me to conceal it.
CARD: No?
Come, I will swear you to 't upon this book.
JULIA: Most religiously.
CARD: Kiss it. [*She kisses the book.*]
Now you shall never utter it; thy curiosity
Hath undone thee; thou'rt poison'd with that book.
Because I knew thou couldst not keep my counsel,
I have bound thee to 't by death.

[*Re-enter* BOSOLA]

BOS: For pity-sake, hold!
CARD: Ha, Bosola!
JULIA: I forgive you
This equal piece of justice you have done;
For I betray'd your counsel to that fellow.
He over-heard it; that was the cause I said

SCENE TWO　　　　　　　　MODERN

CARDINAL: It will bring you closer to your end. I will not tell you. Consider this good advice: it is dangerous to know a prince's secrets. Those that do know them need cold, hard hearts armoured with adamant, the strongest metal, to protect the secrets. Please, be satisfied not knowing them. Consider your weakness (as a woman, prone to gossip). It is easier to keep a secret tied up than to set it loose, just as it's easier to tie a knot than undo one. Mine is a secret which, like a slow poison, will stay inside you and cause your death seven years from now.

JULIA: You're toying with me.

CARDINAL: Enough of this. I will tell you. By my command, the great Duchess of Malfi and her two young children were strangled four nights ago.

JULIA: Oh good heavens! Sir, what have you done?!

CARDINAL: How does it feel? How's this knowledge sinking in? Do you think your chest will be a grave dark and obscure enough to keep this a secret?

JULIA: You've ruined yourself, sir.

CARDINAL: How?

JULIA: It is not possible for me to conceal your secret.

CARDINAL: You don't think? Then I will make you swear upon the Bible to keep it.

JULIA: With all my faith.

CARDINAL: Kiss it. [*She kisses his Bible.*] Now you will never reveal my secret. Your curiosity has been your downfall. The poison I put on that book will kill you. Because I knew you would never be able to keep my secret, I have bound you to it with your death.

　　　　　[*Re-enter* BOSOLA]

BOSOLA: For pity's sake, stop!

CARDINAL: Ah! Bosola!

JULIA: I forgive you for this injustice you have done to me, because I did an equal one to you: I betrayed you and your secret to this man. He overheard it – that was why I said

It lay not in me to conceal it.
　BOS:  O foolish woman,
Couldst not thou have poison'd him?
　JULIA:　　'Tis weakness,
Too much to think what should have been done. I go,
I know not whither.  [*Dies.*]

---

### WHAT'S GOING ON?
*The Cardinal kills his own lover to protect his secrets, and in the most corrupt, Machiavellian, hypocritical way possible — he uses religion as a tool for murder. The first two main characters to be killed are the*

---

　CARD:　　Wherefore com'st thou hither?
285　BOS:  That I might find a great man like yourself,
Not out of his wits, as the Lord Ferdinand,
To remember my service.
　CARD: I'll have thee hew'd in pieces.
　BOS: Make not yourself such a promise of that life
Which is not yours to dispose of.
　CARD:　　Who plac'd thee here?
　BOS: Her lust, as she intended.
290　CARD:　　Very well:
Now you know me for your fellow-murderer,
　BOS: And wherefore should you lay fair marble colours
Upon your rotten purposes to me?
Unless you imitate some that do plot great treasons,
295 And when they have done, go hide themselves i' th' grave
Of those were actors in 't?
　CARD:　　No more; there is
A fortune attends thee.
　BOS: Shall I go sue to Fortune any longer?
'Tis the fool's pilgrimage.
　CARD: I have honours in store for thee.
300　BOS: There are a many ways that conduct to seeming
Honour, and some of them very dirty ones.

SCENE TWO           MODERN

it wasn't possible for me to conceal it.

BOSOLA: Stupid woman — couldn't you have poisoned him?

JULIA: It's a weakness to think about how thing should have been done, when they've already been done. I'm going, and I don't know where.   [*Dies.*]

---

*women, and both are killed as a result of their private lives coming into conflict with the public and political world. Julia attempts to enter the political space by manipulating the Cardinal, but proves unable to meet the challenge.*

---

CARDINAL: Why did you come here?

BOSOLA: In order to find a great man like yourself, not a madman like Ferdinand, who can reward me for my service.

CARDINAL: I'll have you hacked into pieces.
BOSOLA: Don't talk about what to do with my life — it's not for you to determine what happens to it.

CARDINAL: Who brought you here?
BOSOLA: Julia, because she wanted to have sex with me.
CARDINAL: Fine. You know now I am a murderer, just as you are.
BOSOLA: And why do you paint me with the same marble colours that hide your own rotten, corrupt deeds? Are you like those who plan terrible treasonous crimes, and then hide their guilt by killing those who carried out the crimes for them?

CARDINAL: No more. I have a fortune [as in wealth] waiting for you.
BOSOLA: Should I continue pursuing Fortune [as in fate/luck]? It is something only fools do.

CARDINAL: I can reward you with status and privilege.
BOSOLA: There are many roads that lead to apparent honour, and some of them are very immoral.

CARD: Throw to the devil
Thy melancholy. The fire burns well;
What need we keep a stirring of 't, and make
A greater smother? Thou wilt kill Antonio?
  BOS: Yes.
  CARD:      Take up that body.
  BOS:      I think I shall
Shortly grow the common bier for church-yards.

  CARD: I will allow thee some dozen of attendants
To aid thee in the murder.
  BOS: O, by no means. Physicians that apply horse-
leeches to any rank swelling use to cut off their tails, that
the blood may run through them the faster: let me have
no train when I go to shed blood, less it make me have a
greater when I ride to the gallows.

  CARD: Come to me after midnight, to help to remove
That body to her own lodging. I 'll give out
She died o' th' plague; 'twill breed the less inquiry
After her death.
  BOS: Where 's Castruccio her husband?
  CARD: He 's rode to Naples, to take possession
Of Antonio's citadel.
  BOS: Believe me, you have done a very happy turn.

  CARD: Fail not to come. There is the master-key
Of our lodgings; and by that you may conceive
What trust I plant in you.
  BOS:      You shall find me ready. [*Exit* CARDINAL.]
O poor Antonio, though nothing be so needful
To thy estate as pity, yet I find
Nothing so dangerous! I must look to my footing:
In such slippery ice-pavements men had need
To be frost-nail'd well, they may break their necks else;
The precedent's here afore me. How this man
Bears up in blood! seems fearless!

SCENE TWO                    MODERN

CARDINAL: Throw to the devil your miserable concerns about morality. Things are going well, like a fire burning nicely. Why stir it up into smoke by getting concerned about morality? Will you kill Antonio?
BOSOLA: Yes.

CARDINAL: Take up Julia's body.
BOSOLA: I will soon become the ceremonial stand which coffins are placed on at funerals, considering how many dead bodies I've recently held.
CARDINAL: I'll supply you with a dozen assistants to help you murder Antonio.
BOSOLA: Oh, don't do that. Doctors that use leeches to suck infected blood out of their patients cut off the leeches' tails, so the blood runs through them faster. I'm like one of those leeches, but I don't want to get screwed over like them. Assistants will betray me and I'll end up being hanged at the gallows.
CARDINAL: Come to me after midnight to help carry Julia's body to her own lodgings. I'll start the rumour that she died of the plague, which will discourage people from investigating the cause of her death.
BOSOLA: Where's Castruchio her husband?
CARDINAL: He's ridden to Naples, to take possession of Antonio's citadel.

BOSOLA: Believe me, you have done an act [or trick] of goodwill.
CARDINAL: Do not fail to come. Here is the master-key for my lodgings; you can see what trust I have in you by me giving this to you.
BOSOLA: I will be ready. [*Exit* CARDINAL] Oh, poor Antonio. Though you need nothing more than pity, it would be dangerous for me to give it to you! In such a deceptive, slippery place as this I need to be careful of my footing, like men who wear spiked shoes on ice to prevent slipping over and breaking their necks. The example is here for me to follow: I need to be as crafty as the Cardinal. How this man perseveres with shedding blood and seems fearless about it!

Why, 'tis well;
Security some men call the suburbs of hell,
Only a dead wall between. Well, good Antonio,
I'll seek thee out; and all my care shall be
335 To put thee into safety from the reach
Of these most cruel biters that have got
Some of thy blood already. It may be,
I'll join with thee in a most just revenge.
The weakest arm is strong enough that strikes
340 With the sword of justice. Still methinks the duchess
Haunts me: there, there!—'Tis nothing but my melancholy.
O Penitence, let me truly taste thy cup,
That throws men down only to raise them up! [*Exit.*]

### WHAT'S GOING ON?
*That the Cardinal still puts trust in Bosola as his confidante and private assassin seems foolish, and odd, especially after he's just offed Julia in such a devilishly cunning way. But perhaps the possibility that Bosola is now on a quest for moral salvation, rather than material*

Scene Three

[*A church graveyard. Enter* ANTONIO *and* DELIO:]
DELIO: Yond's the cardinal's window. This fortification
Grew from the ruins of an ancient abbey;
And to yond side o' th' river lies a wall,
Piece of a cloister, which in my opinion
5 Gives the best echo that you ever heard,
So hollow and so dismal, and withal

SCENE THREE        MODERN

Well, it makes sense — his sense of security in his high position gives him confidence to do terrible things that will send him toward hell, with only a wall keeping him from it. Well, good Antonio, I will find you, and I will do all I can to keep you safe from these bloodsuckers. It may be I'll join you in a quest for just revenge against them. Justice is on our side and strengthens us. Still I feel as though the Duchess is haunting me. There, there; it's nothing more than my sadness and regret that makes me think so. Oh, penitence, let me fully taste the bitter experience you offer! Penitence — by showing remorse for what we've done wrong and trying to put it right — throws us down by making us suffer, but ultimately raises us up by giving us the chance for salvation.        [*Exit.*]

---

*reward, is impossible for someone so morally illiterate as the Cardinal to consider.*

*Bosola still has some ambiguity about him. Publicly, he promises the Cardinal to carry out his wish and kill Antonio; privately, Bosola swears to keep Antonio safe. Which Bosola does the audience believe?*

---

[*A church graveyard. Enter* ANTONIO *and* DELIO.]
DELIO: That there is the window of the Cardinal's chamber. This building he's staying in was developed from the ruins of an ancient abbey. And over toward the side of the river is a wall, a piece of the old abbey cloister, which in my opinion produces the best-sounding echo you ever heard — so hollow and so dismal,

So plain in the distinction of our words,
That many have suppos'd it is a spirit
That answers.
   ANT:     I do love these ancient ruins.
10 We never tread upon them but we set
Our foot upon some reverend history;
And, questionless, here in this open court,
Which now lies naked to the injuries
Of stormy weather, some men lie interr'd
15 Lov'd the church so well, and gave so largely to 't,
They thought it should have canopied their bones
Till dooms-day. But all things have their end;
Churches and cities, which have diseases like to men,
Must have like death that we have.
  ECHO.     Like death that we have.
  DELIO: Now the echo hath caught you.
20  ANT: It groan'd methought, and gave
A very deadly accent.
  ECHO.     Deadly accent.
  DELIO: I told you 'twas a pretty one. You may make it
A huntsman, or a falconer, a musician,
Or a thing of sorrow.
  ECHO.     A thing of sorrow.
  ANT: Ay, sure, that suits it best.
  ECHO.     That suits it best.
  ANT: 'Tis very like my wife's voice.
25  ECHO.     Ay, wife's voice.
  DELIO: Come, let us walk further from 't.
I would not have you go to the cardinal's to-night:
Do not.
  ECHO. Do not.
30 DELIO: Wisdom doth not more moderate wasting
sorrow
Than time. Take time for 't; be mindful of thy safety.
  ECHO. Be mindful of thy safety.
  ANT: Necessity compels me.
Make scrutiny through the passages

and so clearly distinguishing the words it repeats that many have assumed it's a ghost's voice that answers their own.

ANTONIO: I do love ancient ruins like this. We never tread upon them without setting our foot upon some important history. And without question, here in this open graveyard, which now lies exposed to stormy weather, some men were buried who loved the church so much, and gave so generously to it, that they decided it should house their remains until the end of the world.

But all things come to an end; churches and cities suffer from diseases just as people do, and they wither away and die just like the death that we have.
ECHO: *Like the death that we have.*

DELIO: Now the echo has taken interest in you.
ANTONIO: It groaned, I thought, and had a very deathly tone of voice.

ECHO: *Deathly tone of voice.*
DELIO: I told you it was an impressive echo. You may interpret it as having a voice like a huntsman, or a falconer, or a musician, or a thing of sorrow.

ECHO: *A thing of sorrow.*
ANTONIO: Yes, surely that suits it best.
ECHO: *That suits it best.*
ANTONIO: It sounds very much like my wife's voice.
ECHO: *Aye, wife's voice.*

DELIO: Come on, let's walk away. I don't want you to go to the Cardinal's room tonight. Do not.

ECHO: *Do not.*
DELIO: Human wisdom doesn't do more to lessen a person's debilitating sorrow than time does. Take time for it. Look after yourself.
ECHO: *Look after yourself.*
ANTONIO: I need to do it; I have no choice. Look back on the course

Of your own life, you 'll find it impossible
To fly your fate.
35   ECHO.     O, fly your fate!
  DELIO: Hark! the dead stones seem to have pity on you,
And give you good counsel.
  ANT: Echo, I will not talk with thee,
For thou art a dead thing.
  ECHO.     Thou art a dead thing.
  ANT: My duchess is asleep now,
40 And her little ones, I hope sweetly. O heaven,
Shall I never see her more?
  ECHO.     Never see her more.
  ANT: I mark'd not one repetition of the echo
But that; and on the sudden a clear light
Presented me a face folded in sorrow.
  DELIO: Your fancy merely.
45   ANT:     Come, I 'll be out of this ague,
For to live thus is not indeed to live;
It is a mockery and abuse of life.
I will not henceforth save myself by halves;
Lose all, or nothing.

  DELIO:     Your own virtue save you!
50 I 'll fetch your eldest son, and second you.
It may be that the sight of his own blood
Spread in so sweet a figure may beget
The more compassion.
  ANT:     However, fare you well.
Though in our miseries Fortune have a part,
55 Yet in our noble sufferings she hath none.
Contempt of pain, that we may call our own. [*Exeunt.*]

## SCENE THREE — MODERN

of your own life, and you'll realise it's impossible to escape what fate calls you toward.

ECHO: *Oh, escape your fate!*

DELIO: Listen to that! The lifeless stones of this graveyard take pity on you, and give you good advice.

ANTONIO: Echo, I'm not interested in talking with you, because you are just a dead thing.

ECHO: *You are a dead thing.*

ANTONIO: My Duchess is asleep now, and her little ones; I hope they sleep sweetly. Oh heaven, will I never see her again?

ECHO: *Never see her again.*

ANTONIO: I paid no notice to any of the echo's repetitions except that last one — suddenly, my mind was presented with the clear image of a face folded in sadness.

DELIO: Just your imagination.

ANTONIO: Come, I'll get out of this funk, for to live with such gloomy thoughts is not to live at all. This sort of depression is a mockery and abuse of what life should be like. I won't be able to save myself by going forward half-heartedly. I must be prepared to risk everything, or risk nothing — no in between.

DELIO: Your own goodness will keep you safe! I'll fetch your eldest son, and be your backup. It may be that when the Cardinal sees his family's blood, displayed in such a sweet figure as his sister's son, he will become compassionate.

ANTONIO: Whatever happens, fare well. Although we can't control the miseries fate sends our way, we can control how we endure them. Disregard of pain, considering it beneath us, is a noble response to suffering that we have agency to fashion for ourselves.     [*Exeunt.*]

ORIGINAL     ACT FIVE

*WHAT'S GOING ON?*
*While making their way to the Cardinal's lodgings, still hoping to make friends with him, Antonio and Delio stumble across some spooky stuff. Revenge-tragedies such as this play often featured an element of the supernatural, such as the ghost of Hamlet's father in Shakespeare's play. But whereas for Hamlet, the ghost*

Scene Four

[*Enter* CARDINAL, PESCARA, MALATESTI, RODERIGO, *and* GRISOLAN]

CARD: You shall not watch to-night by the sick prince;
His grace is very well recover'd.
MAL: Good my lord, suffer us.
CARD:   O, by no means;
The noise, and change of object in his eye,
5 Doth more distract him. I pray, all to bed;
And though you hear him in his violent fit,
Do not rise, I entreat you.
PES: So, sir; we shall not.
CARD:   Nay, I must have you promise
Upon your honours, for I was enjoin'd to 't
10 By himself; and he seem'd to urge it sensibly.
PES: Let our honours bind this trifle.
CARD. Nor any of your followers.

MAL: Neither.
CARD: It may be, to make trial of your promise,
When he 's asleep, myself will rise and feign

224

SCENE FOUR          MODERN

*served as a trigger for revenge at the start of the play, the Duchess's ghostly presence comes much later. It shows in part the Duchess's permanence — so strong in life she continues to have presence in death — but also gives a tragic sense of inexorability: her words fail to affect Antonio and won't alter the doomed fate that's soon to come about.*

[*Enter* CARDINAL, PESCARA, MALATESTI, RODERIGO, *and* GRISOLAN — *in the residence of the* CARDINAL *and* FERDINAND]

CARDINAL: You don't need to watch over Ferdinand tonight. He's feeling much better.

MALATESTI: Let us, my lord.

CARDINAL: Oh no, by no means; the noise of all these people, and looking at them all, just makes him feel worse. Please, everyone, go to bed. And if you hear him in a fit of madness during the night, don't get up, I implore you.

PESCARA: Very well, sir; we will not.

CARDINAL: No — I must have you promise, for this is what Ferdinand himself asked for, and he seemed to be in his right mind when he said so.

PESCARA: Our honour is your guarantee in this matter.

CARDINAL: Neither must any of your servants get up in the night.

MALATESTI: They won't.

CARDINAL: It may be, to test the strength of your promise, when Ferdinand's asleep I will rise from my bed and

ORIGINAL ACT FIVE

<sup>15</sup> Some of his mad tricks, and cry out for help,
And feign myself in danger.
   MAL: If your throat were cutting,
I'd not come at you, now I have protested against it.
   CARD: Why, I thank you. [*Withdraws.*]
   GRIS.    'Twas a foul storm to-night.
   ROD: The Lord Ferdinand's chamber shook like an osier.
<sup>20</sup>   MAL: 'Twas nothing put pure kindness in the devil
To rock his own child. [*Exeunt all except the* CARDINAL].
   CARD: The reason why I would not suffer these
About my brother, is, because at midnight
I may with better privacy convey
<sup>25</sup> Julia's body to her own lodging. O, my conscience!
I would pray now; but the devil takes away my heart
For having any confidence in prayer.
About this hour I appointed Bosola
To fetch the body. When he hath serv'd my turn,
<sup>30</sup> He dies. [*Exit.*]

---

### WHAT'S GOING ON?
*After a struggle with his conscience that's such a miniscule aside it's almost comical, the Cardinal makes everyone promise not to come to help if they hear any*

---

   [*Enter* BOSOLA]
  BOS: Ha! 'twas the cardinal's voice; I heard him name
Bosola and my death. Listen; I hear one's footing.

   [*Enter* FERDINAND]
   FERD: Strangling is a very quiet death.
   BOS: [aside.] Nay, then, I see I must stand upon my guard.

SCENE FOUR                    MODERN

pretend to be doing some of his mad tricks, and cry out to you for help, pretending I'm in danger.
MALATESTI: If your throat were being cut, I wouldn't come to help you, now that I've promised not to.
CARDINAL: Thanks very much.    [*Withdraws.*]

GRISOLAN: It was a foul storm we had tonight.
RODERIGO: Ferdinand's room was shaking like a willow tree.
MALATESTI: It was nothing but the devil being kind by rocking his own child in a cradle. [*Exeunt all except the* CARDINAL.]

CARDINAL: The reason I don't want them near my brother is so that at midnight I can carry Julia's body back to her own room without anyone seeing. Oh, my guilty conscience! I would pray now — but I've given too much of myself to the devil to have any confidence in prayer.

It was about this time I told Bosola to fetch the body. When he's served my needs, he dies.    [*Exit.*]

---

*disturbance in the night. Can we guess what's going to happen? The Cardinal is unravelling, and will be undone by his own Machiavellianism.*

---

    [*Enter* BOSOLA.]
BOSOLA: Ha! It was the Cardinal's voice; I heard him mention my name and my death. Listen; I hear someone's footsteps.
    [*Enter* FERDINAND]

FERDINAND: Strangling is a very quiet way to die.
BOSOLA: [*Aside*] Now then — I see I must be very cautious.

35   FERD: What say to that? Whisper softly: do you agree
to 't? So; it must be done i' th' dark; the cardinal would
not for a thousand pounds the doctor should see it.

> [*Exit.*]

BOS: My death is plotted; here 's the consequence of
murder.
We value not desert nor Christian breath,
40  When we know black deeds must be cur'd with death.

> [*Enter* ANTONIO *and* Servant]

SERV: Here stay, sir, and be confident, I pray;
I 'll fetch you a dark lantern. [*Exit.*]
ANT: Could I take him at his prayers,
There were hope of pardon.

BOS: Fall right, my sword!— [*Stabs him.*]
45  I 'll not give thee so much leisure as to pray.
ANT: O, I am gone! Thou hast ended a long suit
In a minute.
BOS:     What art thou?
ANT:     A most wretched thing,
That only have thy benefit in death,
To appear myself.

> [*Re-enter* Servant *with a lantern*]

SERV: Where are you, sir?
ANT: Very near my home.—Bosola!
50  SERV: O, misfortune!
BOS: Smother thy pity, thou art dead else.—Antonio!
The man I would have sav'd 'bove mine own life!
We are merely the stars' tennis-balls, struck and banded
Which way please them.—O good Antonio,
55  I 'll whisper one thing in thy dying ear
Shall make thy heart break quickly! Thy fair duchess
And two sweet children——

ANT:     Their very names
Kindle a little life in me.
BOS:     Are murder'd.

SCENE FOUR               MODERN

FERDINAND: [Talking to no one – or to a hallucination] What do you think about that? Whisper softly – do you agree to it? Okay – then it must be done in the dark. The Cardinal wouldn't want the doctor to know about it, not even for a thousand pounds.     [*Exit.*]

BOSOLA: My death is being plotted. This is my comeuppance for committing murder. We have to disregard all consideration for our just desserts/punishments, and for mercy, when we know that evil deeds have to be set right by killing those responsible.     [*Withdraws.*]

[*Enter* ANTONIO *and* Servant]

SERVANT: Stay here, sir, and please be at ease. I'll fetch you a lantern.     [*Exit.*]

ANTONIO: If I could catch him when he's saying his prayers, there's hope he'll be in the right mood to show me forgiveness.

BOSOLA: Stick into him well, my sword!  [*Stabs* ANTONIO.] I'll not give you the opportunity to pray.

ANTONIO: Oh, I am killed! You have ended a long quest in just an instant.

BOSOLA: Who are you?

ANTONIO: A most wretched thing, who you have helped, in killing me, to finally show my true self – nothing more than a wretch.

[*Re-enter* Servant *with a lantern*]

SERVANT: Where are you, sir?

ANTONIO: Very near my home. – Bosola!

SERVANT: Oh, what terrible misfortune!

BOSOLA: Keep the noise down, or I'll kill you. – Antonio! The man whose life I wanted to save even more than my own! Oh, we are merely tennis balls struck about by the stars for their entertainment with no control over our own lives or actions. Oh, good Antonio, I'll whisper one thing into your dying ear that will make your heart quickly break with sadness, and end your suffering more promptly. Your fair Duchess and your two sweet children –

ANTONIO: Just the mention of their names brings me back to life a little.

BOSOLA:  – They've been murdered.

229

ORIGINAL ACT FIVE

ANT: Some men have wish'd to die
60 At the hearing of sad tidings; I am glad
That I shall do 't in sadness. I would not now
Wish my wounds balm'd nor heal'd, for I have no use
To put my life to. In all our quest of greatness,
Like wanton boys whose pastime is their care,
65 We follow after bubbles blown in th' air.
Pleasure of life, what is 't? Only the good hours
Of an ague; merely a preparative to rest,
To endure vexation. I do not ask
The process of my death; only commend me
To Delio.
70 BOS: Break, heart!
ANT: And let my son fly the courts to princes. [*Dies.*]

BOS: Thou seem'st to have lov'd Antonio.
SERV: I brought him hither,
To have reconcil'd him to the cardinal.
BOS: I do not ask thee that.
75 Take him up, if thou tender thine own life,
And bear him where the lady Julia
Was wont to lodge.—O, my fate moves swift!
I have this cardinal in the forge already;
Now I 'll bring him to th' hammer. O direful misprision!
80 I will not imitate things glorious.
No more than base; I 'll be mine own example.—
On, on, and look thou represent, for silence,
The thing thou bear'st. [*Exeunt.*]

### WHAT'S GOING ON?

*Bit of a whoopsie on Bosola's part. In accidentally killing Antonio, Bosola fulfils the Cardinal's order and could claim his reward. Therefore it's noteworthy in the*

SCENE FOUR　　　　　　　MODERN

ANTONIO: Some men have heard things so sad that they want to die. I am glad that I really will die. I would not want now for my injuries to be treated and healed, because my life has lost all its purpose. In our quest for greatness we are like idle boys whose only concern is how to pass the time; we chase after status and wealth which are just flimsy bubbles blown in the air.

What joy is there in life? Just a few good hours, like those when a fever recedes for a bit, and then it comes back and we must endure more suffering. I don't ask the reason why I've been killed. I only ask that you speak well of me to Delio [or, put Delio in charge of my remains).
BOSOLA: This is so sad!
ANTONIO: And let my son escape the corrupt world of courts and princes.　　　[*Dies.*]
BOSOLA: You seemed to have loved Antonio.
SERVANT: I brought him here to make peace with the Cardinal.

BOSOLA: I don't want you to make any peace with the Cardinal. Take Antonio's body, if you value your own life, and carry him to the room where the lady Julia liked to stay. Oh, my fate moves quickly! I have this Cardinal held against the anvil, and now I'll bring the hammer down on him. Oh, what a terrible mistake! I'll no longer pretend to be something I'm not — whether more glorious or more lowly — instead, I'll be myself. Go, go, servant, and look to be as silent as the thing you're carrying (Antonio's dead body).
　　　　[*Exeunt.*]

---

*next scene that Bosola doesn't even try to do this, and instead pursues his "just revenge". Bosola's killing of Antonio, ironically, cements his moral transformation.*

---

## Scene Five

[*Enter* CARDINAL, *with a book.*]

CARD: I am puzzl'd in a question about hell;
He says, in hell there 's one material fire,
And yet it shall not burn all men alike.
Lay him by. How tedious is a guilty conscience!
5 When I look into the fish-ponds in my garden,
Methinks I see a thing arm'd with a rake,
That seems to strike at me.

[*Enter* BOSOLA, *and Servant bearing* ANTONIO'S *body*]

Now, art thou come?
Thou look'st ghastly;
There sits in thy face some great determination
Mix'd with some fear.
10 BOS: Thus it lightens into action:
I am come to kill thee.
CARD: Ha!—Help! our guard!
BOS: Thou art deceiv'd; they are out of thy howling.
CARD: Hold; and I will faithfully divide
Revenues with thee.
15 BOS: Thy prayers and proffers
Are both unseasonable.
CARD: Raise the watch!
We are betray'd!
BOS: I have confin'd your flight:
I 'll suffer your retreat to Julia's chamber,
But no further.
CARD: Help! we are betray'd!

SCENE FIVE    MODERN

[*Enter* CARDINAL, *with a book — in the Cardinal's room.*]

CARDINAL: I'm puzzled about a question regarding hell. This book says in hell there's just one type of fire, and yet it burns men in different ways and to different degrees. (I wonder, and worry, why not all people are punished equally.) Enough of this book [puts it down]. Ah, how annoying it is to have a guilty conscience! When I look in the fishpond in my garden, I think I see a devil armed with a pitchfork that seems to strike at me.

[*Enter* BOSOLA, *and Servant bearing* ANTONIO'S *body*]

Now, you have come? You look ghastly. There's a look of great determination in your face, mixed with some fear.

BOSOLA: And now that look will become an action. I have come to kill you.
CARDINAL: Ahh! Help! Guards!
BOSOLA: It's no good — they can't hear your howling.
CARDINAL: Stop — I will faithfully share my wealth with you.

BOSOLA: Your pleas and offers come too late.

CARDINAL: Fetch the guards! I am betrayed!

BOSOLA: I have made it so you can't escape. I'll allow you to retreat as far as the place where Julia rests (the grave), but no further.

CARDINAL: Help! I am betrayed!

[*Enter, above,* PESCARA, MALATESTI, RODERIGO, *and* GRISOLAN]

MAL: Listen.
CARD: My dukedom for rescue!
20 ROD: Fie upon his counterfeiting!

MAL: Why, 'tis not the cardinal.
ROD: Yes, yes, 'tis he:
But I 'll see him hang'd ere I 'll go down to him.
CARD: Here 's a plot upon me; I am assaulted! I am lost,
Unless some rescue!
GRIS.   He doth this pretty well;
25 But it will not serve to laugh me out of mine honour.
CARD: The sword 's at my throat!
ROD:   You would not bawl so loud then.

MAL: Come, come, let 's go to bed: he told us this much aforehand.
PES: He wish'd you should not come at him; but, believe 't,
The accent of the voice sounds not in jest:
30 I 'll down to him, howsoever, and with engines
Force ope the doors. [*Exit above.*]
ROD:   Let 's follow him aloof,
And note how the cardinal will laugh at him. [*Exeunt, above,* MALATESTI, RODERIGO, and GRISOLAN.]

BOS: There 's for you first,
'Cause you shall not unbarricade the door
35 To let in rescue. [*Kills the Servant.*]
CARD: What cause hast thou to pursue my life?
BOS:   Look there.
CARD: Antonio!
BOS:   Slain by my hand unwittingly.
Pray, and be sudden. When thou kill'd'st thy sister,
Thou took'st from Justice her most equal balance,

SCENE FIVE      MODERN

> [Enter, on the balcony above, PESCARA, MALATESTI, RODERIGO, and GRISOLAN]

MALATESTI: Listen.
CARDINAL: I'll give my dukedom to anyone who rescues me!
RODERIGO: Blast him; the Cardinal's just pretending to need help!
MALATESTI: It's not the Cardinal.
RODERIGO: Yes, yes it is him. But I would sooner see him hanged than go down to help him.
CARDINAL: There's a plot to kill me! I am attacked! I am lost, unless someone rescues me!

GRISOLAN: He puts on a convincing act, but it's not enough to make me forget my promise.

CARDINAL: The sword's held against my throat!
RODERIGO: If that were true, he wouldn't be able to shriek so loudly.
MALATESTI: Come, come, let's go back to bed. He told us earlier this would happen.
PESCARA: He made us promise not to come down to him. But honestly, his tone of voice does make it sound as if he's not pretending. I'll go down to him, and use brute force to open the locked door to his room.      [Exit above.]

RODERIGO: Let's follow him from a distance, and wait to see how the Cardinal will make a fool of him for going down.   [Exeunt, above, MALATESTI, RODERIGO, and GRISOLAN.]
BOSOLA: You're first to die, to make sure you can't unlock the door and let rescuers in.      [Kills the servant.]

CARDINAL: Why do you want to kill me?
BOSOLA: Look at this. [Shows Antonio's body.]

CARDINAL: Antonio!
BOSOLA: I killed him by accident. Better say your prayers, and quickly. When you killed your sister, you unbalanced the weighing scales of fair Justice,

And left her naught but her sword.

40 CARD: O, mercy!
BOS: Now it seems thy greatness was only outward;
For thou fall'st faster of thyself than calamity
Can drive thee. I'll not waste longer time; there! [*Stabs him.*]

CARD: Thou hast hurt me.
BOS: Again!
CARD: Shall I die like a leveret,
45 Without any resistance?—Help, help, help!
I am slain!

[*Enter* FERDINAND]

FERD: Th' alarum! Give me a fresh horse;
Rally the vaunt-guard, or the day is lost,
Yield, yield! I give you the honour of arms
Shake my sword over you; will you yield?

CARD: Help me; I am your brother!
50 FERD: The devil!
My brother fight upon the adverse party! [*He wounds the* CARDINAL, *and, in the scuffle, gives* BOSOLA *his death-wound.*]
There flies your ransom.
CARD: O justice!
I suffer now for what hath former bin:
Sorrow is held the eldest child of sin.
55 FERD: Now you're brave fellows. Cæsar's fortune was harder than Pompey's; Cæsar died in the arms of prosperity, Pompey at the feet of disgrace. You both died in the field. The pain's nothing; pain many times is taken away with the apprehension of greater, as the tooth-ache
60 with the sight of a barber that comes to pull it out. There's philosophy for you.

SCENE FIVE        MODERN

and left her with nothing but her sword for violent revenge. [In ancient Roman and Greek myth, the figure of Justice is portrayed holding scales and a sword].
CARDINAL: Have mercy!
BOSOLA: Now it's clear your greatness was just on the outside, and you're weak on the inside. You bring about your own downfall faster than the disastrous events around you can drive you down. I'll waste no more time with you. Take this!        [*Stabs him.*]
CARDINAL: You've hurt me.
BOSOLA: Again!        [*Stabs.*]
CARDINAL: Must I die like a defenceless baby hare, without being able to put up any resistance? Help! Help! Help! I am killed!

[*Enter* FERDINAND]

FERDINAND: I hear the battle alarm! Soldier, bring me a fresh horse; prepare the advance-guard, or we'll lose the battle. Surrender! Surrender, and I'll give you the honour of allowing you to keep your weapons. I shake my sword over you — will you surrender?
CARDINAL: Help me; I am your brother!
FERDINAND: The devil! My brother fights with the devil, on the side of the enemy! [*He wounds the* CARDINAL, *and, in the scuffle, gives* BOSOLA *his death-wound.*] There — now your prisoner's dead, you can't get a ransom for him.

CARDINAL: Oh, this is justice! I pay now for the sinful person I have been. A life lived sinfully always breeds sorrow in the end.
FERDINAND: Now you're brave fellows. Caesar's fate was worse than Pompey's, who Caesar killed. Caesar lost a happy, prosperous life when he died; you're like Pompey, only losing your disgraceful lives here on the battlefield. The pain should be nothing to you, because pain seems like nothing when you're thinking about the far greater pain you'll meet with your punishment in hell — just as the pain of an aching tooth suddenly doesn't seem bad when you see

BOS: Now my revenge is perfect.—Sink, thou main
cause  [*Kills* FERDINAND.]
Of my undoing!—The last part of my life
Hath done me best service.
65 FERD: Give me some wet hay; I am broken-winded.
I do account this world but a dog-kennel:
I will vault credit and affect high pleasures
Beyond death.

BOS:      He seems to come to himself,
Now he 's so near the bottom.
70 FERD: My sister, O my sister! there 's the cause on 't.
Whether we fall by ambition, blood, or lust,
Like diamonds, we are cut with our own dust. [*Dies.*]


CARD: Thou hast thy payment too.
BOS: Yes, I hold my weary soul in my teeth;
75 'Tis ready to part from me. I do glory
That thou, which stood'st like a huge pyramid
Begun upon a large and ample base,
Shalt end in a little point, a kind of nothing.

[*Enter, below,* PESCARA, MALATESTI, RODERIGO,
*and* GRISOLAN]

PES: How now, my lord!
MAL:     O sad disaster!
ROD:     How comes this?
80 BOS: Revenge for the Duchess of Malfi murdered
By the Arragonian brethren; for Antonio
Slain by this hand; for lustful Julia
Poison'd by this man; and lastly for myself,
That was an actor in the main of all
85 Much 'gainst mine own good nature, yet i' the end
Neglected.
PES:     How now, my lord!

SCENE FIVE        MODERN

the dentist coming to pull it out. There's some good
philosophy for you.

BOSOLA: Now my revenge will be made perfect. Sink. You
are the ultimate cause — [Stabs FERDINAND] — of my
downfall. This last part of my life is the only part where I've
done things motivated by morality.

FERDINAND: [Thinking he's a horse] Give me some wet hay;
I am short of breath. I think of this world as nothing but a
home for dogs: I am a horse; I will leap over people's
expectations of what will happen to me [i.e. going to hell]
and find great pleasures in heaven.

BOSOLA: He seems more in his right mind, now he's so near
the end of his life.

FERDINAND: My sister, oh my sister! That's the cause of all
this. It doesn't matter if we're brought down by ambition, or
by obsession with our family's status, or by desire, it's
ultimately our own nature and actions that destroy us.
[Dies.]

CARDINAL: You've got your comeuppance, as well.

BOSOLA: Yes. My exhausted soul is ready to leave me; I
cling onto it just with my teeth. I am glad that you, who were
built like a pyramid, on a large, strong base, end up as just
a small point — a kind of nothing.


[Enter, below, PESCARA, MALATESTI, RODERIGO,
and GRISOLAN]


PESCARA: What's going on, my lord?!

MALATESTI: What an awful disaster!

RODERIGO: What on earth happened here?

BOSOLA: Revenge happened; revenge for the Duchess of
Malfi, murdered by her brothers. Revenge for Antonio,
killed by my own hand. Revenge for lustful Julia, poisoned
by the Cardinal. And lastly revenge for myself, who was an
actor in the main part of a play and directed to perform a
role that went against my own good nature — which, in the
end, I neglected to follow.

PESCARA: What's the meaning of all this, my lord?!

CARD: Look to my brother:
He gave us these large wounds, as we were struggling
Here i' th' rushes. And now, I pray, let me
Be laid by and never thought of. [*Dies.*]
90  PES: How fatally, it seems, he did withstand
His own rescue!
MAL: Thou wretched thing of blood,
How came Antonio by his death?
BOS: In a mist; I know not how:
Such a mistake as I have often seen
95  In a play. O, I am gone!
We are only like dead walls or vaulted graves,
That, ruin'd, yield no echo. Fare you well.
It may be pain, but no harm, to me to die
In so good a quarrel. O, this gloomy world!
100 In what a shadow, or deep pit of darkness,
Doth womanish and fearful mankind live!
Let worthy minds ne'er stagger in distrust
To suffer death or shame for what is just:
Mine is another voyage. [*Dies.*]
105  PES: The noble Delio, as I came to th' palace,
Told me of Antonio's being here, and show'd me
A pretty gentleman, his son and heir.

[Enter DELIO, and ANTONIO'S Son]

MAL: O sir, you come too late!
DELIO: I heard so, and
Was arm'd for 't, ere I came. Let us make noble use
110 Of this great ruin; and join all our force
To establish this young hopeful gentleman
In 's mother's right. These wretched eminent things
Leave no more fame behind 'em, than should one
Fall in a frost, and leave his print in snow;
115 As soon as the sun shines, it ever melts,
Both form and matter. I have ever thought
Nature doth nothing so great for great men
As when she 's pleas'd to make them lords of truth:

SCENE FIVE — MODERN

CARDINAL: Look to Ferdinand for an explanation. He gave us these wounds, as we were struggling down here on the floor. And now, please, let me be laid aside and forgotten.
[Dies.]

PESCARA: He managed to prevent his own rescue – with fatal consequences!

MALATESTI: You disgusting murderer – how did Antonio meet his end?

BOSOLA: In a confusion; I don't know how. It was the sort of mistake that seemed contrived, like you would see in a play. Oh, I am gone! We are like the walls of derelict buildings, or tombs, which, being ruins, give no echo. [Once we're ruined/dead, we have no voice or agency to explain ourselves or our actions. Or, we leave no reminder of ourselves/are forgotten.] Fare well. It may be painful for me to die in such a violent way, but it's not unfair. Oh, this gloomy world! It's such a shadowy, dark pit that weak, frightened mankind lives in! Worthy people should never hesitate to suffer death or shame for a just cause. My death is a different voyage: I suffer it as payment for my misdeeds.    [Dies.]

PESCARA: The noble Delio, as I came to the palace, told me Antonio was here, and showed me Antonio's son – a fine gentleman.

[Enter DELIO, with ANTONIO'S son]

MALATESTI: Oh sir, you're too late!

DELIO: So I heard, and was prepared for it. Let's make the best of this terrible situation, and put all our energy into establishing this young man as the successor to his mother, the Duchess. The legacy these wretched brothers leave behind them will be no more than a footprint in the snow, soon melted by the sun. Their lives, and deaths, will leave no lasting impression.

I have always thought nature's greatest gift to people is when she allows them to be voices of truths, such as this one:

Integrity of life is fame's best friend,
Which nobly, beyond death, shall crown the end.

[*Exeunt.*]

---

## WHAT'S GOING ON?

*In contrast to the Duchess's death, the deaths here happen too quickly to carry much emotion, and without much dignity — just a mess of people madly and mutually stabbing each other. This contrast is another way of showing that justice is done.*

*The Cardinal dies reduced to nothing, undone by his attempts to be cunning and struggling with a guilty conscience that should have awakened much earlier in*

SCENE FIVE        MODERN

living an upstanding moral life is necessary for having a good reputation — people with that sort of noble reputation are the ones remembered after their deaths, while they are in heaven.        [*Exeunt.*]

---

*his life. Ferdinand possesses a strange insight in his madness, recognising his brother as the devil and his feelings toward his sister as the cause of it all. Bosola is regretful that it came too late for his actions to be motivated by morality.*

*The Duchess and Antonio's son is brought in to see all this mess, perhaps a bit insensitively, by Delio, who ends the play with a firm message about the importance of living with integrity — people's moral values are central to their reputation and status, both in life and in heaven.*

---